The Complete
Lincoln Cent
Encyclopedia

Shane M. Anderson

Published by

700 E. State Street • Iola, WI 54990-0001
Telephone: 715/445-2214

Please call or write for our free catalog.
Our toll-free number to place an order or obtain a free catalog is 800-258-0929
or please use our regular business telephone 715-445-2214
for editorial comment and further information.

Library of Congress Catalog Number: 96-76701
ISBN: 0-87341-445-4
Printed in the United States of America

All photos except the one of Mr. Brenner are courtesy of the
Museum of the American Numismatic Association.

Snap-Loc™ is a trademark of Whitman Coin Products.
Scan:Align™ is a trademark of American Business Concepts.

DEDICATION

This book is dedicated to all collectors
of Lincoln Cents . . . past, present and future.

CONTENTS

FOREWORD

In current U.S. numismatics, there is no more enduring, popular, or prolific coin than the Lincoln Cent. It is a tribute to a man whose greatness has grown, as have the fruits of his labor. It is doubtful we would have the Lincoln Cent without the skill and determination of Victor D. Brenner and an influential friend of his, Theodore Roosevelt.

Many of today's coin collectors "cut their teeth" taking cents out of circulation and plugging them into penny boards, always in hope of finding the "1909S VDB" that has remained undetected in change. There are many ways to collect Lincoln Cents; they vary based on the reach of your pocketbook and imagination. Year sets, varieties, errors, proofs, matte and/or brilliant, from well-worn to brilliant red specimens—there are many ways to group America's most collectible coin. Varieties, both new and old, are continually being discovered to join the ranks of the 1909S/S, the 1922 "No D," the 1946D/S, and the 1955, 1969, 1972, and 1995 doubled die obverses.

Since 1909, the United States has seen many changes. Our coinage, as portrayed by the cent, reflects some of these changes. The initials' controversy, wartime alloys, the replacement of the wheat ear reverse, the 1982 alloy change, and the inevitable abolition of the denomination are some of them.

This book represents a documentation of facts and varieties, and an investigative probing into this unique series. It can only add to the enjoyment and fascination of collecting the Lincoln Cent.

J. P. Martin
Authenticator and Resident Numismatist
American Numismatic Association

PREFACE

The greatest advantage of numismatics is that you can mold and shape it to fit you. You can collect what you want, how you want—there is no right or wrong way to assemble a collection.

Numismatics offers you the opportunity to be a casual collector or an avid numismatic scholar. Learning is the very heart of coin collecting. Discovering a new variety, or a lost and forgotten one, is the greatest thrill a collector can experience. However, in order to discover a variety it is vital to increase your knowledge of whatever facet interests you. The information is neverending. No one knows everything about Lincoln Cents, or about the designer who created the most spectacular profile bust to ever grace our coinage.

This book was written to bring together as many facts as possible in one concise reference book. Even this book is not complete, for there will always be one more variety, one more interesting die crack that a collector like you will discover.

I hope this book will enlighten and entertain you, as it has for me in putting it together.

Shane M. Anderson

ACKNOWLEDGMENTS

There are several people whose help has made this book possible. The staff at the American Numismatic Association: Robert J. Leuver, for allowing the inclusion of the official ANA Grading Standards for Lincoln Cents; J. P. Martin, for writing the foreword and providing valuable information on counterfeit detection; Barbara J. Gregory, for her endless support and encouragement; and the rest of the ANA staff for contributing the outstanding photographs that accompany the text. Others who have laid the groundwork not only for this book, but several others, include the following: Walter Breen, R. S. Yeoman, William Sheldon, Kenneth Bresset, and especially Alan Herbert, whose research and writing have eliminated almost all of the ambiguity and myths surrounding the minting process.

Finally, I would like to thank my wife for her encouragement and enormous help with research and typing, and the folks at Krause Publications for their encouragement and continuing dedication to this hobby.

HISTORY OF MODERN COINAGE

The first coins (if one could call them that) were actually pre-weighed lumps or nuggets of electrum, a naturally formed alloy of gold and silver. These "coins" were first widely used in Lydia, now known as Turkey, in 650 B.C. The "coins" were stamped with an official seal of a merchant to indicate that the purity and weight had been verified. It did not take long, however, before enterprising citizens clipped small pieces from the "coin" and used them as a medium of exchange. Something had to be done to stop this practice, other than reweighing the "coin" prior to every transaction. The irregular size and shapes of the electrum made it very difficult to determine if the piece was clipped or shaved—thus evolved coins.

The first real coins were made by melting metal in a crucible and casting it in the shape of a small round disc. This disc, or blank, was later reheated to soften the metal so the coiner could easily make an impression on the face with a simple punch and a rapid blow of a hammer. These coins had a similar size and shape, which reduced, but not eliminated the practice of clipping. Many of these early coins are very crude in comparison with modern-day coins, with off-center strikes and incomplete or lightly struck devices being the norm rather than the exception.

These early coins were often used to honor the leaders of the nations that stamped the coins. Some even depicted current newsworthy events of the day, and so people were kept informed of events hundreds of miles away.

The first coins minted in the New World were minted out of sheer necessity. England at the time wanted to keep the Colonies on a barter economy, which meant the Colonists had to barter for all of their transactions. In Boston, popular bartering items were fur, fish, musket balls, rifles, and Indian "wampum" (an Indian form of currency). In the Southern colonies, people preferred to barter with tobacco. This created a trade war, as tobacco was more plentiful in the South than in the North, and was not an even form of exchange between the Colonies. Colonists were not paid in gold or silver for their exports; rather, they were paid in bills of exchange that were payable only in the Colonies. With such a system in place, no real money (gold or silver) ever had to leave England to pay for the Colonists' exported merchandise.

Colonists were required to pay taxes in gold or silver to the King of England. Any gold or silver the Colonists happened to acquire through foreign trade with other countries had to be shipped to England, thereby leaving them with no real currency. This enabled England to keep its stranglehold on the economy.

In 1652, during the chaotic reign of Oliver Cromwell, the Massachusetts Bay Colony decided to coin its own currency. A mint was established in Boston and the silver coins minted there are known collectively today as Pine Tree Schillings. All of these coins have the same date (1652) even though they were of different denominations and minted for over thirty years. This was done in an attempt to avoid reprisal from England, as minting coins in the Colonies was considered an act of treason punishable by imprisonment or death. These problems for the Colonists were major contributors to the American Revolution.

Wanting to rid itself of English influence, America decided to develop its own monetary system after the Revolutionary War. It wasn't until 1792 that the United States Mint became established. The idea of a national mint was first proposed by a patriot and financier of the Revolution, Robert Morris. Many of the coins minted through the early half of the nineteenth century had French rather than English influences in their design. It wasn't until the early 1900s that an American coin depicted an actual person, let alone a president.

A LOOK AT VICTOR D. BRENNER

The Lincoln Cent has become the most widely collected coin the U. S. Mint has ever produced. On August 2, 1909, the day it was first issued, people lined the streets around the Federal Reserve Bank in San Francisco to get the first new coin that honored a president instead of Liberty. In New York City, a crowd of people swarmed the Wall Street Subtreasury, all wanting to purchase what would surely become a family keepsake. In the first two days of issue, over seven hundred thousand coins were issued.

The Lincoln Cent was not the first choice to replace the aging Indian Head Cent designed by James B. Longacre. The first choice was a design created by Augustus Saint-Gaudens, but the talented artist died in 1907 before completing the task. Saint-Gaudens originally intended to include a flying eagle on the obverse, similar to the one used briefly from 1856 to 1858. Instead, he opted to use a left-facing Liberty with a feathered bonnet, and reserve the flying eagle for the reverse of his twenty-dollar gold coin. The reverse he designed for the cent was very cluttered, unlike the Lincoln Cent's elegant, yet simple, design.

The man responsible for the new Lincoln Cent was a talented medalist named Victor David Brenner, an immigrant from Shavli, Lithuania, who was born on June 12, 1871, under the name of Victoras Barnauskaus. When Brenner was ten his father taught him the art of engraving and seal-making, which were popular at the time. At age thirteen, Brenner became a full-time apprentice at his father's workshop where he carved broaches, headstones, jewelry, seals, and stamps that were pressed into molten wax to seal letters.

In 1889 in the town of Kovno, at the urging of his jealous co-workers (whom he constantly out-performed), Brenner prepared a seal for a local government official. The undertaking was against the law in that country, and the young engraver was convicted of counterfeiting. He was tried and sentenced to a Siberian labor camp. Before he was to be transported there, he fled the country with the help of his brother and sister and came to America. In 1906 Brenner became a naturalized U.S. citizen and opened a modest studio. That same year Brenner joined the American Numismatic Association and became member #841.

In 1908 Brenner was asked to create a plaquette and subsequent medal to celebrate the upcoming centennial of Lincoln's birth. On the plaquette he created is the best likeness of Lincoln ever produced—whether it be photograph, sculpture, or otherwise. At first glance the Lincoln Centennial Medal looks identical to the plaquette; however, there are a few subtle differences. The plaquette is in higher relief and contains more detail around the eyes and trunk, and gives the viewer an appreciation for Lincoln's tall stature. The plaquette is considered by many to be Brenner's finest creation.

In the spring of the same year, Brenner was asked to create a Panama Canal service medal to be awarded to workers with two years of outstanding service. On the obverse was the bust of then president Theodore Roosevelt and on the reverse were three ships navigating the canal. While Roosevelt was sitting for Brenner in his New York studio, he noticed the almost completed plaster pattern plaquette of Lincoln and commented on how much he liked it.

After returning to Washington, the influential president helped Brenner win a commission to redesign the Indian Cent. The obverse of Brenner's new cent was an exact replica of the bust on the Centennial Medal, but naturally in lower relief. As a result of coinage production requirements, some of the depth and detail were sacrificed. Brenner first opted to use a reverse copied from the French two-franc piece, but when Mint Director Leach discovered this, he immediately rejected Brenner's design. Brenner was undaunted by this

The new reverse of the Lincoln Cent was simple, yet bold, with the words ONE CENT surrounded by two sheaves of Durham wheat.

seemingly insurmountable setback. He went back to his studio and designed a new reverse to complement his well-received obverse.

The new reverse was simple yet bold, with the words "ONE CENT" surrounded by two sheaves of Durham (spaghetti) wheat. At the bottom the artist spelled out his full last name, BRENNER. Feeling that his name was too prominent on the reverse, the Mint substituted V.D.B. in place of the artist's name, but even this was controversial.

Coinage production of the new Lincoln Cent did not start until June 1909. President Roosevelt did not want the motto IN GOD WE TRUST to appear on the coin—he felt it was irreverent and in poor taste—but before the final dies were completed, Taft succeeded Roosevelt and refused to approve the design without it. The master die had to be reworked, which held up production.

On August 5, 1909, coin production was halted a mere three days after the first coins had been issued. Chief engraver Charles Barber was ordered to Washington D.C. and told to remove the too-prominent initials on the reverse of the Lincoln Cent. When an offer was made to place a modest "B" on the truncation of the shoulder on the obverse as a way of pacifying the artist, Barber protested vehemently on the grounds, one would assume, that he did not want anyone to confuse Brenner's work with his own. Barber said it would be much easier and two weeks faster to remove all the initials from the hub and leave the dies alone. By September, Brenner's initials were removed and the few cents that did contain those three letters are now the most popular in all of numismatics. The coin was easy to strike and its stunning obverse has kept it in production for over eighty years. With billions being minted each year, Brenner's bust of Lincoln as featured on the one-cent coin holds the honor of being the most reproduced work of art in the world.

In February 1917, Charles Barber died and the Mint lost its strongest opponent to the Lincoln Cent. The Mint quietly replaced Brenner's initials on the coin, this time on the trunk of Lincoln's bust.

At the time he designed the Lincoln Cent, Victor David Brenner was a respected medalist with more than seventy medals and plaquettes to his credit.

President Roosevelt did not want the motto IN GOD WE TRUST to appear on the Lincoln Cent, but before the final dies were completed Taft succeeded Roosevelt and refused to approve the coin's design without it.

Victor David Brenner died in a New York hospital on April 5, 1924, at the age of fifty-three. His name will always be synonymous with the Lincoln Cent, which is not only a tribute to a beloved president, but also to a great medalist: V.D.B.

(This article written by the author first appeared in the October 1993 issue of *The Numismatist*, "V.D.B.: Behind the Initials," and is reprinted here courtesy of *The Numismatist*, official publication of the American Numismatic Association, 818 North Cascade Avenue, Colorado Springs, CO 80903-3279.)

DIE MAKING

The process of making Lincoln Cents has not changed much since it was first introduced in 1909. This is especially true for the process of making the dies that are used to create the images of the coin. The process of making a die is very labor intensive and time consuming. The first thing the designer has to do is come up with a design that meets all of the requirements needed for that coin. The main devices (i.e. portrait) include the placing of the date and mintmark; the required phrases "Liberty," "In God We Trust," "E Pluribus Unum," and "The United States Of America"; and the denomination "One Cent." A designer must take all of these elements and create a coin that is easy to strike and appealing at the same time—a daunting task.

The design is sketched and approved before the designer creates a model in plastic (actually made of "Plastilene," which is often still called "wax"). The plastic model is roughly twelve inches in diameter and contains the same relief that will be on the coin. When everyone is satisfied, the plastic model is placed on a Janvier "pantographic" reduction lathe, which transfers the plastic pattern to a hub that is the same size and relief as the finished coin. Developed in 1907, the Janvier lathe has a tracing tool that follows the relief and contours of the "wax model" and transfers the detail in miniature to the other end of the machine, which has a stylus that actually cuts the design into a soft steel blank.

The steel blank, called the master hub, is then annealed, or heat treated, to harden it, and placed into a hydraulic press. Another soft steel blank is carefully placed and aligned underneath the master hub. The master hub is pressed into the soft steel face of the master die two or more times, resulting in a negative or incuse design. As a labor saving measure, prior to 1985 for proof coins and 1990 for circulating coins, the mintmark was added to the master die after the hubbing operation rather than to the working die.

The master die is used to make working hubs, which again have the same relief as the finished coin. These working hubs are used to make hundreds of working dies, which have negative images and actually strike the coins. The working hubs are placed into presses, then heated (softened) die blanks are placed directly underneath. The working hub is pressed into the die blank, then the die is removed and reheated. The process is repeated two or more times to bring up full relief. It was during this process in 1955 that one of the working dies was slightly rotated in the press before the final impression was made. This slight rotation caused the 1955 doubled die variety.

Prior to the early 1990s, only the main branch in Philadelphia had a die shop. It produced all of the Lincoln Cent working dies for the branch mints in Denver, San Francisco, and West Point. Today the Denver Mint also produces working dies in its new addition.

LINCOLN CENT
MANUFACTURING PROCESS

Modern day Lincoln Cents start out as an alloy of 99.2% zinc and .8% copper. The two elements are melted and mixed together in large furnaces, then the molten metal is poured from crucibles into large molds where it is allowed to cool in the form of rectangular ingots. The ingots are rolled under very high pressure into thin strips, which are wound up into coils and weighed to verify the alloy mixture. These large coils are annealed in a furnace to soften the metal before they are unrolled and cleaned with wire brushes, then drawn through two more rollers under very high pressure to achieve the correct thickness for blanking. The coils are then fed through large presses containing "gang punches" that punch the planchets out of the strip in a matrix that minimizes waste. The planchets drop onto a vibrating screen conveyor, or "riddler," where any clippings or clipped planchets will be separated from the good planchets. Planchets of normal size will be allowed to pass through holes in the bottom of the riddler into a gondola. The planchets are then tediously cleaned prior to being chemically plated with a thin layer of copper. Previously, all of these steps were done in-house at the mint. Today the U.S. Mint buys planchets from companies like the Ball Corporation in Tennessee, eliminating the need to expend valuable time and resources on operations that can be done more efficiently on the outside.

When they are received by the mint, Type I planchets have their edges upset or raised to form the basis for the rims. This is done in an upsetting machine. The planchets are fed out of hoppers and into narrow grooves smaller than the diameter of the planchet. A revolving drum rotates the planchet against a fixed metal fence, forcing the metal from the outside edge toward the center of the planchet while forming the rim. The planchet is now quite a bit thicker toward the center than at the rim. When the planchet is struck by the dies, this mound of metal will cold flow, radiating outwards toward the edges, producing a sharper and fuller strike in the center, where it is very difficult for the metal to flow otherwise.

Type II planchets are annealed in large slowly rotating drums inside of ovens at approximately 1400 degrees, which softens the metal so the planchets can be more easily struck by the dies. The planchets are placed in the oven on one end and are mechanically transferred to the other end at a specific rate. If one gets stuck inside the annealing drum, a sintered coating can form on its surface. This coating is metal dust or powder that accumulates and is baked onto the surface of the planchet. This dust is caused by the constant metal-to-metal contact of the planchets as they tumble inside of the drum. The planchets are then dumped into a quenching bath, which maintains the metals' softer state and removes any residual dust or powder.

Next, the planchets are fed through coining presses that have up to four die pairs. Each of these coining presses can turn out slightly over six hundred coins per minute. Not all of the presses at the mint facilities are that fast. In fact, the "modern Mint" still employs coin presses that predate World War II and can only turn out 120 coins per minute. The Mint is continuing to gradually replace these antiques with new modern presses.

Regardless of the age or style of the press, all presses utilize some form of mechanical feed mechanism to place the planchets between the upper and lower dies. Most of these incorporate feed fingers that strip off the bottom planchet from a feed tube and drag the planchet into position, then quickly retract with a previously finished coin. On the faster multidie presses, a rotating plate with equally spaced holes around the outer diameter strips off a planchet and rotates the planchet between the dies. The benefit of the dial plate is that the dies actually strike the coin through the plate openings, eliminating the motion of removing the mechanism before or during the strike. The lower, or anvil, die ejects the coin back into the dial plate and is rotated out as a new planchet is rotated in.

There are actually three dies used to strike a coin: the upper die, the lower or anvil die, and the collar. Typically the planchet is placed on the anvil die. The upper die is attached to a ram and is forced downwards against the planchet. The metal is thicker in the center than it is on the edge and is therefore under stress sooner. This metal compresses and flows outwards under the immense pressure and into the cavities of the design in the upper and lower dies. The collar retains the metal to keep it from flowing out from between the two dies as they come together. All of this occurs in a fraction of a second.

A sampling of the coins stamped from each die pair is inspected by the press operator to make sure it meets the Mint's stringent criteria. The remaining coins are escaped into large bins, and after being weighed, are dumped into large storage hoppers or gondolas. From here the coins are hauled by semi-trucks to the twelve Federal Reserve Districts to be dispersed to banking institutions.

PROOF LINCOLN CENT
MANUFACTURING PROCESS

Proofs are made slightly different from regular business strikes. Modern day proofs have a mirror field and frosty, or cameo, devices. To achieve this end result, great care must be taken to avoid damaging the planchets before they are struck. The planchets used for proof cents are sorted and placed into a large vibrating bowl filled with small elongated steel pellets. This process, known as burnishing, creates a bright surface on the planchets, but not a highly reflective finish. The planchets are then placed onto a conveyor belt that passes through a specially designed annealing furnace. The mint cannot use the standard revolving annealing drum because as the drum rotates, the planchets would strike against each other. When the planchets come off the conveyor belt they are sent down a chute and accumulated into a large bin. This is done to avoid as much metal-to-metal contact as possible.

Dies used to make proof coins are handled much more carefully than common working dies because a lot of work goes into a proof die. The proof dies are made in a similar fashion as regular dies, but before the initial hubbing process, each die face is chrome-plated and carefully polished. After the hubbing process the dies are sorted and prepared by sandblasting the devices and the rest of the design. This process results in the frosty devices found on the actual proof coin. (Prior to 1985, it was just before this stage that the S mintmark would have been added.) A protective covering is placed over the field to prevent damage. The die is complete once the fields are polished with diamond dust to smooth out any flow lines or imperfections.

The 1990S "No S" proof is a very rare and unique type of minting variety. When the hubs were being prepared, a mint employee forgot to "punch" the mintmark into the hubs (a practice that had become standard operating procedure in 1985).

The next step, actually striking the coins, is what really separates a proof coin from a business strike. Business strikes are fed into large presses that can contain up to four die pairs. The coins are fed into the machine at the rate of 140 per minute and are ejected into large bins. Proof coins, on the other hand, are fed one at a time into a press that is solely used for striking proofs. The coin is not ejected after the first strike like a business strike, but rather remains in the collar for a second or even third strike to bring out the full details. Once the coin is finally ejected it is released into an accumulating system where it is transported to another riddler, which separates out defective planchets. The Mint used to rely on keen-eyed inspectors to visually inspect and pick all of the defects off a conveyor system as it went by, but with cutbacks, the Mint is relying more heavily on mechanical sorting devices such as the riddler. The Mint has even looked at computer-controlled vision systems, which have been widely accepted in the automation industry for years, and could discern good and bad strikes and other oddities as the coins go by. After inspection, the coins are delivered to the assembly line where mint employees actually put the proof sets together by hand. The assemblers are also the final inspectors before the coin is sonically sealed in its plastic holder.

Matte proofs are coined in a similar fashion but do not have mirror-like fields and frosty devices; rather, the whole surface of the coin is granular in appearance. This is accomplished by striking the coin two or more times, and then *after* the final strike the surface of the coins are processed to achieve the desired look. A lot of the matte proof Lincoln Cents are heavily toned or stained, caused by the sulfur in the yellow envelopes that the mint used to house the matte proofs. It is often difficult to distinguish a matte proof from a regular uncirculated business strike due to the surface condition of the matte process. Genuine matte proofs will have a very sharp rim on the outer diameter of the coin and the edges will be sharp and square rather than beveled. The detail on the obverse will be much crisper than a regular business strike. Many of the catalogues list a 1917 Matte Proof—these coins were clandestinely made and therefore not real mint-issued coins.

In the mid-1950s, dealer speculation on the aftermarket price of proof coins drove the mintages skyward. Dealers encouraged friends, family, and customers to purchase as many sets as they could to be resold hopefully for a modest profit. The Mint produced proof coins based on the number ordered, and with more proof coins being ordered, more were being made, eventually saturating the marketplace. This practice was also done in the early 1980s, with the same effect. Proof coins were being resold through major department stores such as Sears and Kmart, again saturating the market.

In 1983 the Mint came out with a marketing strategy that was used to sell more proof coins at higher prices. This strategy was the introduction of the Prestige Set—a handsomely packaged proof set in a padded case. These were heavily promoted by the Mint and cost a good deal more than the standard proof set for the same year. As a collector of proof Lincoln Cents, remember you are buying the coin(s) in the package, not the package itself.

MINTING VARIETIES AND ERRORS
OF LINCOLN CENTS

A variety can occur at any stage of the minting process and can be caused by mechanical or human error. There are four categories of minting varieties: planchet (P), die (D), striking (S), or official mint modification (O).

PLANCHET (P) ERRORS

A planchet error (P) can occur at any time up to the point it is fed into the coining press. These errors or varieties include the following:
1) Wrong or improperly mixed alloys
2) Damaged or defective planchets
3) "Clipped" or incomplete planchets
4) Laminations or split planchets
5) Planchet stock
6) Sintered planchets
7) Unstruck planchets

1) Alloy errors often occur due to incomplete mixing of the elements that form the alloy. This results in planchets that are streaked, that flake, or are brittle. Another possible error is that the wrong mixture of elements were combined to form the alloy, resulting in the wrong specific gravity of the coin.

Lincoln Cents made after 1982 often show bubbling or blistering on the surface of the coin. This is caused by improper rinsing of the planchet after it was plated with copper. These blisters are caused by residual chemicals left on the planchet after the plating process. Under the right conditions (humidity and moisture) the chemicals will react and form blisters or discoloration on the surface of the coin. These should not be confused with a planchet error, but are rather an inherent vice of the plating process.

2) Damaged or defective planchet errors can occur at any point up to the actual striking of the coin. A damaged planchet will have rounded areas of damage caused by the striking of the coin. Damage caused after striking the coin will be sharp or jagged.

3) "Clipped" or incomplete planchets result when the hitch feed mechanism on the blanking press causes the web to misfeed as it is indexed through. A "clipped" planchet occurs when the punch comes down off-center of the intended area and overlaps with an area that has already been punched. This type of error can easily be identified by the half-moon shape or straight clipped (occurs when the punch comes down on the end of the web) area of the coin that is missing. The detail next to the clipped area will be lacking and will be rounded into the clipped area.

4) Laminations or split planchets occur when the strips are rolled under heavy pressure to form a) coils, or b) the proper blanking thickness of the strip. Dirt or trapped gasses may be picked up and cause the metal to strip into thin layers or laminations. This may occur before or after the planchet is struck. It is considered a split planchet if more than twenty percent of the weight of the coin splits off, including all or most of one face.

5) Planchet stock which is of the wrong material may be fed through a blanking press. Although this error is very uncommon for Lincoln Cents, a few well-publicized planchet stock error coins have been reported (i.e. the 1943 copper cent).

6) Sintered planchets are by far the most elusive type of planchet error, but are not valuable. This occurs when the planchet picks up a layer of metallic dust while it is in the annealing drum longer than normal. The heat from the annealing process is enough to bond the layer of metallic dust to the surface of the planchet, forming a discolored area which may stay in place during the strike.

7) Unstruck planchets sometimes get mixed up with coins that have already been struck. There are two types of unstruck planchet errors. A Type I error is a planchet that has not been through the upsetting process to form the rims; a Type II planchet error has had its edges upset, but hasn't been struck. Type I planchet errors are easily faked and are not commonly collected by variety collectors.

DIE (D) VARIETIES

Die varieties (D) are by far the most collected variety in all of numismatics. Die varieties or errors are defined as any alteration or change of the die surface or design up until the moment of impact of the die pair. Die varieties are repeated on every coin that is struck and therefore are not a singular incident.

There are six major classifications of die varieties:
1) Engraving
2) Hubbing
3) Mintmark varieties
4) Die cracks and die breaks
5) Dents, gouges, scratches, or polishing
6) Die and collar clashes, and design transfer

Rotated hub doubling is responsible for the 1955 (shown at right), 1972, 1984, and 1995 doubled die Lincoln Cents, to name just a few.

1) Engraving varieties consist of any intentional or accidental change of the design itself. An example of an engraving variety would be the 1940s Lincoln Cent with a plain or crosslet "4" in the date.

2) Hubbing varieties only occur during the hubbing process. A popular example of this type of variety would be all overdates after 1901, such as the 1942/1 dime. Another form of hubbing variety is rotated hub doubling. Rotated hub doubling is responsible for the 1955, 1972, 1984, and 1995 doubled die Lincoln Cents, to name just a few. These varieties are caused when the hub or die is slightly rotated or axially off-center between impressions, or as in the case of the 1942/1 dime, the wrong hub was used.

All true hubbing varieties will produce a raised and rounded second image, unlike die bounce, or die clatter, which produces raised, flat, "shelf-like" doubling. Die bounce occurs after the first strike of the coin, when the die(s) may contact the coin a second time, leaving a faint flat impression.

Hubs, like dies themselves, are prone to crack or even break during use. Examples of hub breaks would include the 1956 Lincoln Cents with a chip out of the "6" and the 1936 Lincoln Cents with a missing leg of the "R" in LIBERTY.

3) The two types of mintmark varieties are repunched mintmarks and overmintmarks. A repunched mintmark occurs when two punches of the same letter are placed over the top of one another. An example of a repunched mintmark would be the 1909S over horizontal S. An overmintmark is defined as a mintmark from one branch being punched over the mintmark from another. An example of an overmintmark would be the 1944D/S.

4) Die cracks and die breaks are very common die varieties. A die crack is a raised irregular *line* of coin metal and a die break is a raised irregular *area* of coin metal. When a die deteriorates from use, the surface of the die may crack and metal from the planchet is forced into the die crack, just like it is forced into the incuse areas of the die. A die break occurs when a piece of the face of the die actually breaks, but is captured so the area that broke is in a different position on the die, resulting in it being in a different position on the surface of the coin. When chips and small die breaks occur in the die around letters or numerals, they are referred to as "clogged" letters or numerals. When a large piece of the die breaks away and is not captured, the coin made from that die is often referred to as a "cud," and has a portion of the design missing entirely.

The 1909S over Horizontal S Lincoln Cent is an example of a repunched mintmark. A repunched mintmark occurs when two punches of the same letter are placed over the top of one another.

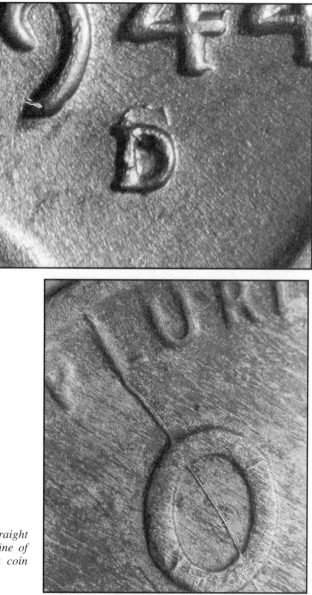

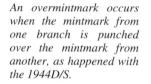

An overmintmark occurs when the mintmark from one branch is punched over the mintmark from another, as happened with the 1944D/S.

A close-up of the 1922 reverse straight die crack. A die crack is a fine line of raised metal on the surface of a coin caused by a crack in the die.

5) Dents, gouges, scratches, or polishing: Dies are not impervious to damage—the constant striking of coins takes its toll. Die scratches are the most common form of die damage. As the die wears, it will be polished with an abrasive to minimize the appearance of wear. The amount of polishing done on a die can have a great impact on the appearance of the coin. Severe die polishing can remove, reduce, or enlarge the design, depending on how much metal is removed from the die.

6) Die and collar clashes, and design transfer: Severe damage can occur to the dies if they come together without a planchet between them. The image of one die can cut into the

field of the opposing die, leaving an outline of the image. When the next planchet is struck, the outlined image, as well as the intended image, will be struck into the coin. This phenomenon is called "die clash" and is relatively common.

On several of the early Lincoln Cents a similar type of image transfer can be seen. This is called Internal Metal Displacement Phenomenon or "IMDP." The image of the obverse die is transferred through the coin to the reverse die due to the constant pounding of the dies. This is also known as the "Ghost of Lincoln."

STRIKING (S) ERRORS

Striking errors or varieties (S) can only occur at the time of final impact of the dies with the planchet. Under extreme pressure provided by the coin press, the metal is cold flowed into the recesses of the designs on the die pairs. Metal that has cold flowed in this manner creates flow lines, which we call luster, on the coin's surface.

There are eight striking variety categories that relate to Lincoln Cents:
1) Die adjustment strikes
2) Indented, brockage, and counterbrockage strikes
3) Strikes through abnormal objects
4) Strikes on abnormal objects
5) Double or multiple strikes
6) Collar errors
7) Misaligned and rotated dies

1) Die adjustment strikes: When they are placed into the coin press, new dies must be set up and installed correctly. The installation process may involve several weak strikes on planchets to test the alignment of the die. These weak strikes may show only a faint trace of the design.

2) Indented, brockage, and counterbrockage strikes: These types of strikes occur when a second planchet or struck coin gets between a planchet and the dies. When the planchet is struck, an indentation of the coin or planchet will be transferred. These are known as indented strikes.

A brockage strike occurs when a struck coin is partly or completely between the planchet and the die. The most common form of this variety is when a coin sticks to the upper die and another planchet is escaped underneath it. As the coin stuck to the top die thins out after repeated blows, the impression of the top die will be transferred through the coin, but will be weak and blurred.

A counterbrockage strike occurs when a struck coin acts as a die and imparts an enlarged and distorted relief image onto the planchet during the striking process.

3) Strikes through abnormal objects: Through dubious or inadvertent actions, just about anything from cloth, wire, paint, even springs, can get between a die and the planchet. When the press strikes the coin, the abnormal object will leave an impression or even become embedded in the coin.

4) Strikes on abnormal objects: Again whether intentional or by accident, electrical box knock-outs, wrong planchets, washers, and even nails have been struck at the mint. Several years ago a mint employee struck several nails with coin dies and smuggled them out of the mint only to have them confiscated by the Secret Service.

5) Double or multiple strikes: A double strike occurs when a coin fails to be ejected from the die completely and gets struck a second time. This form of double strike will force all raised areas of the first strike back down to field level on both sides of the coin. The only parts of the design from the first strike that will be in relief are those that happen to fall under the design of the second strike.

6) Collar errors: The collar is a heavy steel ring, often called the third die, that fits over the bottom, or anvil, die. It is mounted on springs. The purpose of the collar is to keep the coin metal from spreading outwards when the coin is struck. With the outer perimeter of the coin sealed, the coin metal will flow into the incuse portions of the dies. If for some reason the collar is below its normal position, the coin metal will flow out over the top of the collar and create a flange on the coin. This is called a flanged partial collar. If the collar is all the way down during a strike, then the resulting coin would be classified as a broadstrike. Broadstrike coins are typically thinner and larger in diameter than usual. Sometimes when the collar is all the way down, the planchet may not be centered in the die. If this planchet is struck, it is called an off-center strike.

7) Misaligned and rotated dies: Sometimes dies (typically the top dies) can become misaligned and strike just one side of the coin off-center. Dies can also rotate if the setscrew used to hold them in orientation loosens with wear, or if the die itself breaks. Typically, most U.S. coins have a 180 degree rotation between the obverse and reverse. If a die rotates it is called a rotated reverse, even though either the top or anvil die may be involved.

OFFICIAL MINT MODIFICATION (O)

Official mint modification (O) is the final category of varieties and errors. The few Lincoln Cents that fall under this heading are the matte proofs of 1909-1916. Matte proofs were struck with specially prepared dies on select planchets. These proof coins were further treated by the mint *after* the final strike in the coining press. Typically, anything that happens to a coin once it has been struck is considered to be damage. However, in the case of matte proofs it is this post processing that distinguishes them from the rest of the field.

1909 VDB Matte Proof Obverse

STORAGE AND HANDLING OF COPPER, BRASS, AND BRONZE COINS

Unfortunately, the single most overlooked aspect of numismatics is the proper handling and storage of coins. Due to improper handling, more coins have forever lost their collector appeal. As every aspiring collector learns, there is a right and wrong way to hold or house a coin.

Copper, brass, and bronze coins such as Lincoln Cents are actually very fragile. Any coin you handle should be held between the thumb and index finger, touching only the edge. Your hands contain an acidic oil that can and usually does leave a fingerprint that can destroy a coin's collector value in a relatively short period of time. The acid reacts with the copper and dissolves the protective patina on the coin's surface.

Always make sure your hands are clean and dry before examining your coins. I highly recommend the use of cotton or latex gloves whenever handling a coin. I have found that latex gloves provide more control over small coins than cotton, but cotton works fine also. Both types of gloves can usually be found at pharmacies or specialty stores. The smaller the coin, the more easily it can roll in your fingers, and as a result you can leave oil in the rim or even on the field. The oil will tarnish the coin and slowly ruin its appeal.

Never talk when standing over your coins and don't hold them close to your mouth when viewing them. Every time you exhale, you expel tiny droplets of moisture that can land on the coin's surface and cause it to become pitted. It is also very important to examine your coins over a soft padded area. This is to prevent damage to the coin if you were to accidentally

An example of a "pitted" coin. These small unsightly holes in the coin's surface are usually a result of chemical reactions.

drop it. Use a clean, folded up, cotton bath towel, or better yet, a jeweler's pad, which can be purchased at most any hobby or craft store.

As mentioned earlier, copper coins such as Lincoln Cents are actually very fragile. Even though they are made of metal, they can scratch and dent easily. Proper handling goes hand in hand with proper storage. Of all the coins you can collect, copper coins are by far the most easily damaged. Several potential problems that can occur with copper coins are spotting, pitting, tarnishing, and the accumulation of verdigris, the greenish crust typically seen on the field near the rim. If not cared for properly, copper coins are difficult to maintain in original condition. The number one enemy of copper coins is the combination of heat and humidity. When at a coin show or dealer's retail store, it is best to look at as many coins as you can in order to find the one that is the most problem-free. This will pay off when it comes time to upgrade or sell.

There are several good ways to house and store your collection. However, some coin holders may contain chemicals that can damage the very coins they were intended to protect. The worst of these chemicals is a plasticizer known as polyvinyl chloride (PVC). When subjected to heat and moisture, PVC can break down chemically and produce hydrochloric acid. This, in turn, reacts with the copper and produces verdigris on the coin's surface. PVC is generally not used today in the production of flips.

A "flip" is a common, inexpensive 2" x 4" rectangular plastic holder that has pockets into which you place the coin. The only way to place or remove a coin from one of these holders is to let the coin slide against one side of the plastic. This type of holder is just that, a holder. It offers very little in the way of protection. Another holder, also known as a "flip," is a 2" x 4" cardboard holder with various size cutouts and a clear transparent mylar backing that is folded over itself and stapled to form a 2" x 2" holder. However popular they are with dealers, they offer little or no protection for copper coins. The staples used to hold the flips together may rust or scratch other coins. Another potential problem is that the cardboard contains sulfur, and tiny flecks of cardboard may gravitate to the coin's surface and form carbon spots. Carbon spots, the tiny black spots often found on coins, are actually isolated areas of oxidation that form when moisture reacts with the sulfur and the metal of the coin.

Coin albums with cutouts that you press coins into, such as the ever popular blue folders or albums that have sliding mylar covers over the coins, are not made to protect, but rather to hold coins. All cardboard albums contain sulfur and those with the sliding mylar covers can actually scratch the highest areas of your coins, no matter how careful you are. Do not be lulled into a sense of security by these folders for full red uncirculated cents. These types of holders are perfect for housing inexpensive collections of circulated cents. The best

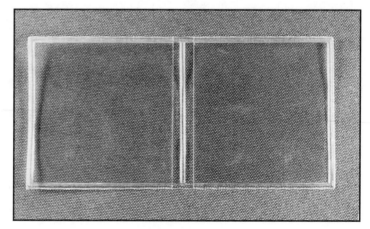

A "flip" can hold your coins, but unfortunately offers very little protection for copper coins.

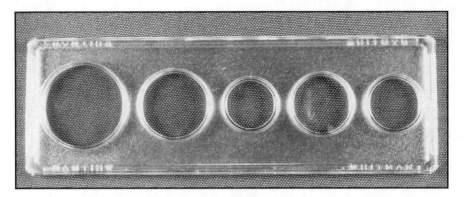

The best method to store your uncirculated coins is to encase them in an airtight holder made of inert plastic.

method to store your uncirculated coins is to encase them in an airtight holder made of inert plastic. This is very true for high grade specimens. Whitman Coin Products offers the Snap-Loc holder, consisting of two polystyrene squares that snap together, making a virtually airtight seal. The plastic squares compress slightly against the rims of the coin, preventing them from rotating or rattling in the holder.

After you decide in what manner you will store your coins, you will have to decide where to store your collection. All coins should be stored as far away from heat and humidity as possible. Avoid storing your collection in an area that has wild temperature swings, such as a basement or attic. The best place to house your collection is a climate-controlled safety deposit box. Several banks now offer this service to their customers. Do some investigating and see which bank near you provides this service.

Housing an expensive collection in your home can be very risky. Most home owners insurance policies do not cover numismatic collectibles as part of their standard coverage. Call your insurance agent or the American Numismatic Association in Colorado Springs, Colorado (800-467-5725) for information on insuring your collection. If you decide to house your collection at home, take a few preventative measures. Do not leave your coins out in the open; keep them hidden or better yet, locked up. There are several good inexpensive safes on the market today. Some safes labeled as "fireproof" or "fire resistant" can actually damage your coins. Between the inner and outer walls is a solid chemical that can "sweat" moisture in the right conditions. Investigate several safes such as gun safes or other similar safes without the dangerous chemicals. If you decide to buy a safe or already have one, conceal it! A visible safe is an open invitation to a thief.

Once a month it is a good idea to pull out your collection and check its condition. Make sure the coins are not being accidentally subjected to adverse climates or conditions without your knowledge. Remember, an ounce of prevention is worth a pound of cure.

GRADING LINCOLN CENTS

Grading coins, whether they are well worn or uncirculated, takes practice. Grading coins is not a true science, but rather a mix of opinions, experience, and art. As Ken Bresset said, "Grading is really very simple. All you need is four things: (1) a good magnifying glass, (2) a good light, (3) a good memory, and (4) 20 years of experience. In order to grade effectively, one must look at a lot of coins, especially when you are trying to determine if the particular piece is the 'normal' way you usually find that date or if it is above average." Grading coins does not have to be intimidating for the beginner. All collectors, regardless of their current knowledge or stature, started grading coins the same way. The most popular saying in numismatics today is "buy the book before you buy the coin," which holds very true, especially for grading. Get practice grading pocket change before going out to buy an uncertified MS64 1922 "No D" cent. Practice, practice, practice—with enough practice and patience you will soon be able to tell the difference between an AU and an MS.

Grading coins is the easiest way to become accustomed to looking at coins with a specific objective in mind. Whether it be grading or authenticating, knowing what to look for, as well as how to look for it, is the key to becoming a knowledgeable collector. To view coins, I recommend a 10X power loupe. It is a magnifying glass that enlarges the object ten times its normal size. The loupe design folds in on itself, protecting the lens surfaces during storage. The best light to use in grading a coin is a 100 watt incandescent light bulb at approximately three feet from the coin's surface. According to the official ANA grading standards, "To grade a coin, hold it between your fingertips over a soft padded area at an angle so that light from the source reflects from the coin to your eye." Rotate the coin and look at the entire coin—both the obverse and reverse, as well as the edge. Don't forget to look at the coin without magnification to get an overall appearance of the surface and luster of the coin. If the coin is common or inexpensive and has a few flaws, search for other coins of the same type and date. Find the most problem-free coin you can. Remember, as in other aspects of life, you get what you pay for. There are no bargains in numismatics.

What is grading and why is it important? For dealers as well as collectors, a coin's value as a collectible is directly related to the coin's grade. A coin's grade is essentially a number that quickly denotes the coin's condition. Describing a coin as Very Fine (VF-20) is a lot easier than saying that the head on the obverse is flat-looking with some detail remaining, the ears and bow tie are worn but clearly defined, and the lines in the wheat ears are worn but clearly separated. This shorthand is almost universally accepted by most dealers and collectors.

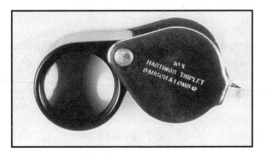

The loupe design folds in on itself, protecting the lens from damage.

There are five categories that you need to consider when grading a coin: surfaces, luster, color, strike, and overall eye appeal. Four of the five categories are included in this numismatic shorthand: surfaces, luster, strike, and overall eye appeal. Color is not so much a grade as a condition, and as such is typically included as a suffix, for example VF-20 RED.

Surface refers to the number of scratches, nicks, or other imperfections on a coin's obverse, reverse, and rims. Luster is a classification that is typically reserved for Mint State coins. It denotes the amount of reflectivity off the coin's surface, and is the result of microscopic concentric flow lines that radiate out from the center of the coin. The flow lines are caused by the cold flowing of metal during the striking of the coin. If a copper coin reflects light in a circular pattern it is said to have "full mint luster." On heavily circulated coins, traces of original mint luster can often still be seen, typically in the recesses of the motto and legend.

If a copper coin is full red in color, but shows no trace of luster, then the coin was probably processed. Processed copper coins are easily distinguishable from specimens that have original luster and color. The flow lines on the surface of a coin are very minute raised lines that can be easily removed by using a pencil eraser, through whizzing, or by dipping the coin. Dipping copper coins should never be undertaken, regardless of how diluted the solution may be. The acid in the solution will quickly remove the flow lines from the entire surface of a coin.

In 1977 the American Numismatic Association came out with a book titled *The Official American Numismatic Association Grading Standards for United States Coins*. This book has gone through several reprints and is used today by most dealers and collectors for surface and luster grading.

To further confuse or clarify the situation, depending on your viewpoint, copper coins are also categorized or graded by the color of the coin. These categories are Red (R), Red-Brown (RB), and Brown (B). Copper coins are always in a state of transition from full red color to total blackness. This may occur gradually over years, or even decades, or as short as a few days in moist conditions. There is no scientific procedure to determine the color of a copper coin; it is a subjective opinion. A coin that exhibits most of its red color with a few very small flyspecks of isolated toning, or a slight toning over the entire surface of the coin, may be considered by some as Red or even Red-Brown. The best way to categorize a copper coin is by the overall appearance of the coin, both the obverse and reverse. If the overall appearance of a coin is Red, then it should be categorized as such. If a coin is almost full Red on one side and almost full Brown on the other, it should be categorized as Red-Brown.

Copper coins, even in slabs or holders, can still change color over a period of time as short as a few months or years. If a coin was graded or categorized as Red a few years ago, it may over time become Red-Brown or even fully Brown. This is why you should never purchase a copper coin that has been slabbed sight unseen. There is no way to prevent or totally stop this color transition on copper coins. The only defense is proper handling and storage, which should slow down the process.

Strike is the amount of detail that is passed on to the coin from the dies when the coin is actually struck at the mint. Some coins, especially those minted in the 1920s, are typically weakly struck, so that all of the design may not have been transferred to the coin. A weakly struck coin can actually be produced by two means: The die may be heavily worn or polished so it will not impart all of the expected details onto the coin, or the pressure used to stamp the coin may be less than what it takes to bring up all of the detail. With experience it will be easy to discern the amount of detail that is generally expected from a given mint and year, and grade accordingly.

The last category in grading coins is overall eye appeal. A coin can have a different appearance to different people. Some collectors look at different regions on the coin than those listed in *The Official ANA Grading Standards for United States Coins*. Lighting and different magnification also play a critical role as to how a coin looks and is graded. Was the coin seen or graded in "natural" light or under fluorescent lights on the bourse? Different magnification also makes a difference—too strong of magnification and all the problem areas overwhelm the coin as a whole; not enough magnification and the slight blemishes on the coin will not be noticed until it is time to trade up or sell.

The official grading standards for coins use a numerical scale of 3 (About Good) to 70 (theoretically perfect Mint State coin). This scale was first proposed by a large cent collector by the name of Dr. William Sheldon in the 1800s and is often referred to as the "Sheldon Scale." The scale has gone through a lot of changes, as the criteria for most grades have been tightened quite a bit in the last decade. What may have been graded MS-65 in 1985 may only be an MS-63 today.

Coins are divided into three categories for grading purposes: circulated, uncirculated, and proof. Circulated coins can be anywhere on the scale from 3 (About Good) to 55 (About Uncirculated). Uncirculated and proof coins range from 60 to 70 (not including impaired proofs). Remember that the term "proof" is not a grade, but rather a type of coin.

Below are the official ANA grading standards for Lincoln Cents. It is impossible in the scope of this book to cover every facet of coin grading. For a more in-depth and complete guide to grading coins, I highly recommend *The Official ANA Grading Standards for United States Coins,* Fourth Edition, put out by the American Numismatic Association (800-467-5725). The book also features quality black and white photographs accompanying each grade description.

THE OFFICIAL ANA GRADING STANDARDS FOR LINCOLN CENTS

(Courtesy of the American Numismatic Association)

MINT STATE *Absolutely no trace of wear.*

MS-70 *Uncirculated*
A flawless coin exactly as it was minted, with no trace of wear or injury.
Must have full mint luster and brilliance or light toning. Any unusual die or planchet traits must be described.

MS-67 *Uncirculated*
Virtually flawless, but with very minor imperfections.

MS-65 *Uncirculated*
No trace of wear; nearly as perfect as MS-67 except for some small blemishes.
Has full mint luster, but may be unevenly toned or lightly fingermarked. A few barely noticeable nicks or marks may be present.

MS-63 *Uncirculated*
A Mint State coin with attractive mint luster, but noticeable detracting contact marks or minor blemishes.

For a more in-depth guide to grading coins, I recommend the Official A.N.A. Grading Standards for United States Coins, *Fourth Edition published by the American Numismatic Association.*

MS-60 *Uncirculated*
A strictly uncirculated coin with no trace of wear, but with blemishes more obvious than for an MS-63. May lack full mint luster, and surface may be dull or spotted.

ABOUT UNCIRCULATED *Small trace of wear visible on highest points.*

AU-58 *Very Choice*
Has some signs of abrasion: high points of cheek and jaw; tips of wheat stalks.

AU-55 *Choice*

    Obverse: Only a trace of wear shows on the highest point of the jaw.

    Reverse: A trace of wear on the top of the wheat stalks.

    Almost all of the mint luster is present.

AU-50 *Typical*

    Obverse: Traces of wear show on the cheek and jaw.

    Reverse: Traces of wear show on the wheat stalks.

    Three-quarters of the mint luster is still present.

EXTREMELY FINE *Very light wear on only the highest points.*

EF-45 *Choice*

    Obverse: Slight wear shows on hair above the ear, the cheek, and on the jaw.

    Reverse: High points of wheat stalks are lightly worn, but each line is clearly defined.

    Half of the mint luster still shows.

EF-40 *Typical*

    Obverse: Slight wear shows on hair above the ear, the cheek, and on the jaw.

    Reverse: High points of wheat stalks are lightly worn, but each line is clearly defined.

    Traces of mint luster still show.

VERY FINE *Light to moderate even wear. All major features are sharp.*

VF-30 *Choice*

    Obverse: There are small flat spots of wear on the cheek and jaw. Hair still shows details. Ear and bow tie slightly worn but show clearly.

    Reverse: Lines in wheat stalks are lightly worn but fully detailed.

VF-20 *Typical*

    Obverse: Head shows considerable flatness. Nearly all the details still show in the hair and on the face. Ear and bow tie worn but bold.

    Reverse: Lines in wheat stalk are worn but plain and without weak spots.

FINE *Moderate to heavy even wear. Entire design clear and bold.*

F-12

    Obverse: Some details show in the hair. Cheek and jaw are worn nearly smooth. LIBERTY shows clearly with no letters missing. The ear and bow are visible.

    Reverse: Most details are visible in the stalks. Top wheat lines are worn but separated.

VERY GOOD *Well worn. Design clear but flat and lacking details.*

VG-8

    Obverse: Outline of hair shows, but most details are smooth. Cheek and jaw are smooth. More than half of the bow tie is visible. Legend and date clear.

    Reverse: Wheat shows some details and about half of the lines at the top.

GOOD *Heavily worn. Design and legend visible but faint in spots.*

G-4

    Obverse: Entire design well worn with very little detail remaining. Legend and date are weak but visible.

    Reverse: Wheat is worn nearly flat, but is completely outlined. Some grains are visible.

ABOUT GOOD *Outlined design. Parts of the date and legend worn smooth.*

AG-3

    Obverse: Head is outlined with nearly all details worn away. Legend and date readable, but very weak and merged into rim.

    Reverse: Entire design partially worn away. Parts of wheat and motto merged with the rim.

SELECTING MAGNIFYING GLASSES (LOUPES) AND MICROSCOPES

As stated in Chapter 8, to view coins I recommend a 10X power loupe, which is a strong-powered magnifying glass that enlarges the object ten times its normal size. The loupe design folds in on itself, protecting the lens surfaces during storage.

If you are very interested in numismatics, a good stereomicroscope is an excellent invest-ment as well. There are a lot of minor repunched mintmarks and minor doubled dies that are only visible with strong magnification. If you are interested in purchasing a scope, I highly recommend a stereomicroscope. This is a magnifying device with two independently adjustable eye pieces, and magnification of anywhere from 10X to 60X. Look for a scope with high-quality glass optics, and coarse and fine focal adjustments.

The most important part of any microscope is lighting. The higher the magnification, the more light is required due to the focal lengths of the optics. The best light I have found is an incandescent ring light. This light is an accessory that clamps around the base of the lower optic lens. The light bulb is approximately three inches round and provides an almost continuous 360 degree light source that is adequate up to about 30X magnification.

I do not recommend scopes that rely on reflected light via a small gimbaled mirror below the slide table. This type of scope is not intended for viewing a solid object such as a coin, but rather material placed on a clear slide. The light is reflected from its source up through the slide and to the viewer's eye. If you try to view a coin through one of these types of scopes, all you will see is a nice eclipse.

Take your time when selecting a scope. Good stereomicroscopes start at about $500 . Find a scope that fits your style of collecting. You typically do not need anything over 30X magni-fication. Scopes with a higher magnification need a *lot* of light and almost perfect optic lenses for good viewing. You can also get scopes with a camera mount to take crisp clear pictures of your coins with almost any 35mm camera. Find a scope that is comfortable to look through for an extended period of time, and you will discover a whole new facet to collecting.

Another option for collectors who own a computer is to scan their coins. A scanner is a peripheral device that takes a "snapshot" of an image placed in front of the aperture. Two types of scanners are available—handheld and flatbed. Handheld scanners are relatively inexpensive and typically do not have the resolution or clarity of a flatbed. I recommend a flatbed scanner because you can scan several raw coins or up to twelve encapsulated coins in one setting.

To scan a coin with a handheld scanner, I highly recommend a device such as Scan:Align, manufactured by American Business Concepts. This is a device with a clear acetate sheet that rests on top of the image or coins to be scanned and prevents them and the scanner itself from moving unwantingly when operating the scanner. On a flatbed scanner, gently place the coin(s) on the glass surface and close the lid.

I recommend you scan with the highest possible resolution setting; this will provide much more detail and contrast. Using a flatbed scanner with 900 dpi (dots per inch) resolution, I was able to scan 120 raw coins in one pass and still maintain clarity even when the image was later magnified by four hundred percent. You will have to play around with the settings to find out what works best for your particular setup.

Scanning coins is a great way to document the coins in your collection, as your entire collection can be saved on your hard drive or any data media. A visual record can also be used for insurance purposes or can be viewed by another collector several hundred miles away via the Internet without the coin ever leaving your possession.

COMPARISON BETWEEN RAW AND SLABBED COINS

Coin clubs across the country have engaged in a debate over slabbed, encapsulated coins versus raw or unslabbed coins. "True" collectors say that encapsulated coins are "investor coins" and not true collectibles. Encapsulated coins have several advantages and some disadvantages over raw coins.

Slabbed coins are coins that are graded and sonically sealed inside inert plastic holders to protect the coin and the integrity of the assigned grade. Slabbed coins, if done by a respected third-party grading service, are a good purchase for beginning collectors who are intimidated by the prospect of buying a coin and having to rely solely on their own grading judgment. Even seasoned veterans purchase slabbed coins when buying very expensive specimens or ones they are unfamiliar with.

In the hobby of collecting Lincoln Cents or any other copper coinage, slabs have numerous advantages over raw coins. Copper is a very reactive element and is prone to damage much more readily than nickel, silver, or gold. Copper coins are by far the hardest to keep in Mint State. A copper coin sealed in a holder is much less susceptible than a raw coin to damage attributed to humidity and climate. I highly recommend inert airtight plastic holders for anyone who collects Lincoln Cents. Through your local coin dealer you can purchase slabs or holders such as Whitman Coin Products' Snap-Loc holder, which is made out of two 2" x 2" clear inert plastic pieces that snap together, creating a virtually airtight seal around the coin. Several people have commented that you can't pick up and "feel" a coin if it is encased in plastic, but you should never "feel" a copper coin anyway without some type of protection against damage, such as cotton or latex gloves. The acid in your skin reacts very quickly with copper, easily destroying its collector appeal and value.

If you are dead set against slabbed coins, you can always break the coin out of its holder and store it however you wish. A word of caution if you decide to break out a coin: The plastic holders splinter, creating very sharp corners or points that can easily damage you or your coins.

Slabbed coins do have some distinct disadvantages over raw coins. It is true that when you pick up a slab, you're picking up a piece of plastic with a coin stuck in its center. You can view the obverse and the reverse, but not the edge as you could with a raw coin. Also, raw coins are much easier to weigh than slabbed coins. (Weighing a coin that is slabbed and getting an accurate reading is virtually impossible, as the weight of the plastic varies from holder to holder even from the same grading service.) Another disadvantage of slabbed coins, or coins in any type of holder, is that you're looking through clear plastic to see the coin. The viewing area of the holders or slabs can scratch, become dirty, or distort the view of the coin underneath.

The final disadvantage of slabbed coins is that it costs typically between $25-$30, plus insurance, to get a coin graded by a third-party grading service. Whether you elect to have a coin slabbed or purchase a slabbed coin from a dealer, you will end up paying for that service. As a result, all slabbed coins from the top grading services command a premium over raw coins, even for the same date, grade, and so on.

The debate over slabbed versus raw coins will continue as long as third-party grading services exist, but do not be intimidated by what others think or say. Remember, there is no right or wrong way to put together a collection. Besides being assured a fairly accurate grade and a greater degree of protection, slabbed coins are no better or worse than raw coins.

BUYING AND SELLING COINS

The best piece of advice anyone can receive is "Buy the book before you buy the coin." This statement also holds true if you plan on selling the coin. Most collectors generally purchase their coins from coin dealers. Most large cities have several coin dealers listed in the Yellow Pages of the phone directory. These dealers may be full or part time, retail, mail order, or a combination. A dealer is in business for one primary reason, to make a profit. This is not a bad thing, for without dealers where would we get our coins?

There are some guidelines that should be followed whenever you decide to do business, whether it be with a coin dealer or any other retailer. Find out how long the dealer has been in business. Does he or she stand behind what they sell with an offer to buy back any merchandise that is later proven defective or even counterfeit? Find out if the dealer offers a return policy on coins purchased. Typically, most dealers will offer a refund on coins they sell as long as they are still in the original packaging. A few dealers will charge a small "restocking" fee: this is a fairly common business practice with most specialized retailers, not just coin dealers. Finally, find out what other customers have to say about the dealer before you give him or her your business.

Establishing a good relationship with a dealer can yield some surprising results. If a dealer knows what your interests are and what you typically purchase, he or she may keep a watchful eye out for a coin that you need. Dealers can also be a great source of information on a particular subject.

Most dealers sell and buy based on a fixed price list, often called "The Gray Sheet." This list is used by most dealers, which gives you the option to shop around to find the best possible coin, already knowing approximately how much it is going to cost.

Some of the best places to buy or sell coins are regional or national coin shows and conventions. These shows generally have several dealers that specialize in just Lincoln Cents, and may have hard-to-find, problem-free coins. Shop around, walk the bourse, look at what dealers have to offer before actually settling on any particular dealer. Find the most problem-free coin that you can for the best price. One piece of advice that applies not only to dealers at a coin show, but to retail merchants as well: **NEVER** interrupt a transaction between the dealer and another buyer. The dealer will be more than happy to help you after the transaction is complete.

Buying coins sight unseen, especially copper coins, is a risky proposition. If a telemarketer or a dealer advertising in a publication refuses to send you a written return policy **BEFORE** sending you the coins, then find another dealer. For example, quite a few years ago I called on a local retail dealer for the first time to purchase a key Lincoln Cent. He said he could order a slabbed MS-64 Red coin from his supplier, but I needed to put down a $100.00 deposit to prove I was interested in actually purchasing the coin. A few days later he informed me that my coin had arrived and I could come pick it up. When I saw the coin, it had a very unattractive fingerprint on the obverse, and was actually Red-Brown, not Red as I had requested. The slab stated that the grade was indeed MS-64 Red, but the fingerprint and the discoloration did not match the grade it was assigned. I told the dealer the coin was unacceptable. He then told me that the $100.00 deposit was nonrefundable. It was an expensive lesson, but I learned to be cautious with any new dealer and to ask for a written return policy. If they know you, most dealers can occasionally get a coin into their store on an approval basis without a deposit, so you can see what you are buying.

Before trying to sell a coin or an entire collection, you should be aware of its value. Do not rely on what a dealer or potential buyer says it is worth. Do not be offended if dealers refuse to buy your coin or collection: it may be because their regular customers specialize in different coins or they may already have too many in stock. Depending on their situation and the coin's resell potential, most dealers will offer anywhere from seventy to seventy-five percent of the going retail price.

Another option for selling (or buying) your coins is through an auction house. Some auction houses specialize in coins and collectibles. For a list of these contact the American Numismatic Association in Colorado Springs, Colorado. If you decide to sell your coins by auction, write or contact the company **BEFORE** sending any coins. Learn how they want the coins packaged for shipment and what type of paperwork needs to be included. Auction houses work off a commission basis, and it is a good idea to get the company's commission fees and reserve bid policy in writing before submitting any coins.

A quick word on investing in Lincoln Cents: In the mid to late 1980s, several firms were stating that investing in ultra-high grade common date coins from any series would yield high profits, as much as ten percent per year. This is very far from the truth. Some key coins from a few series have dramatically risen in value for the short-term, but Lincoln Cents are the backbone of the hobby, and as such are collector rather than investor coins. If you are debating whether to invest in ultra-high grade (MS-67 or higher) common date Lincoln Cents, keep in mind that copper coins are by far the most difficult to preserve and thus lose their value the easiest. You must ask yourself if owning the highest grade 1988D Lincoln Cent is worth the thirty dollars it would cost just to get it "slabbed" when you can buy the same raw coin for ten cents at the local coin shop. Ultra-high grade, common date Lincoln Cents offered as premium quality (PQ) have no resale market, not even from the dealer who sold them to you in the first place!

Always remember to buy a coin because you like it, not because a dealer said it was a good deal. A coin with a grade that is unquestionable when you purchase it will in all likelihood be easier to sell or trade in the future. Good luck and most of all, have fun!

UNIVERSAL RARITY CHART

On the following page is the Universal Rarity Chart based on Q. David Bowers' method first published in *The Numismatist* in June of 1992. It is often difficult to relate mintage figures to a coin's actual rarity or abundance. Mintage figures tell us how many coins were minted, but do not give any indication as to how many survive today. It is possible to estimate with a fair degree of accuracy the number of coins that survive based on a large enough sample. With the advent of third-party grading services, it is now fairly easy to obtain the large, relatively unbiased sample that is required. However, many people have removed coins from their holders and resubmitted them in the hopes they would get a higher grade. This practice lends to discrepancies and inaccuracies of population reports put out by third-party grading services. One way of getting around this problem is to assign a grade or number for a range of coins submitted.

As an example, John Smith resubmitted his MS-64 1909 VDB ten times in the hopes that his coin would be graded to his advantage. Let's say there have been 3,000 Mint State 1909 VDB coins submitted for grading. John Smith resubmitted the same coin ten times, skewing the statistics to report 3,010 coins submitted. So, the actual numbers listed by the population reports can be misleading. Most third-party grading firms that publish population reports go to great lengths to provide accurate information.

The "Universal Rarity Scale" consists of ranges or divisions that progress mathematically, with each category containing approximately one-half as many members as the previous category. If we assign a category or division number from the same scale to Mintages, Mint State Rarity, and Spectral Rarity, we can use the tolerance amidst the high and low numbers of each category to offset multiple submissions of the same coin.

If we look at the total number of Mint State 1909 VDB coins submitted (as an example we'll use 3,000), and assign a number to the range—i.e. R19 is assigned for the range of 2,294 to 3,441—John Smith's influence on the data has been greatly diminished. This is not a foolproof method when it comes to the actual rarities of the series, but overall, its effectiveness is satisfactory.

The numbers for the Mint State Rarity and Spectral Rarity classifications are based on the latest cumulative census provided by three of the leading third-party grading services: Professional Coin Grading Service (PCGS), Numismatic Guarantee Corporation (NGC), and ANACS.

I chose 262 million as the cutoff for the Universal Rarity Chart, so any coin with a mintage in excess of that was not assigned a Mintage Rarity. The problem with using numbers provided by third-party grading services is that most people do not submit inexpensive coins of ultra-high mintages, so the later common date cents appear to be rare when, in fact, just the opposite is true.

UNIVERSAL RARITY CHART

R1	1 Known Specimen
R2	2
R3	3
R4	4 - 6
R5	7 - 9
R6	10 - 15
R7	16 - 24
R8	25 - 37
R9	38 - 57
R10	58 - 87
R11	88 - 132
R12	133 - 199
R13	200 - 300
R14	301 - 451
R15	452 - 678
R16	679 - 1,018
R17	1,019 - 1,528
R18	1,529 - 2,293
R19	2,294 - 3,441
R20	3,442 - 5,163
R21	5,164 - 7,746
R22	7,747 - 11,620
R23	11,621 - 17,431
R24	17,432 - 26,148
R25	26,149 - 39,233
R26	39,234 - 58,836
R27	58,837 - 88,255
R28	88,256 - 132,384
R29	132,385 - 198,577
R30	198,578 - 297,867
R31	297,868 - 446,802
R32	446,803 - 670,204
R33	670,205 - 1,005,307
R34	1,005,308 - 1,507,962
R35	1,507,963 - 2,261,944
R36	2,261,945 - 3,392,917
R37	3,392,918 - 6,785,836
R38	6,785,837 - 10,178,755
R39	10,178,756 - 15,268,134
R40	15,268,135 - 22,902,201
R41	22,902,202 - 34,353,303
R42	34,353,304 - 51,802,956
R43	51,802,957 - 77,704,436
R44	77,704,437 - 116,556,656
R45	116,556,657 - 174,834,986
R46	174,834,987 - 262,252,481

DATE BY DATE SYNOPSIS

1909-1995

The following section contains a date by date synopsis of the most common minting varieties of Lincoln Cents from 1909 to 1995. For each variety listed you will find five designations below the variety heading: Mintage, Mintage Rarity, MSR (Mint State Rarity) or PR (Proof Rarity) for proof issues, Spectral Rarity, and Classification. Each of these designations contain a wealth of useful information.

Mintage is the actual number of coins minted for a particular date and mint. For some varieties it is impossible to tell precisely the actual number of coins minted. For these conditions I refer you to the base heading for that date, which lists a mintage that encompasses all subsequent varieties for that date and mint. In some instances I included the Mint's own official estimates as the mintages; other times they are estimates from leading numismatists.

Mintage Rarity is the number correlating the actual mintage number with the Universal Rarity Chart.

MSR or Mint State Rarity designates the total cumulative quantity of Mint State (MS-60 or above) coins submitted to three of the leading third-party grading services. The numbers shown are the respective rarity numbers from the Universal Rarity Chart.

Spectral Rarity designates the total cumulative quantity of Mint State coins with full red color or luster submitted to three of the leading third-party grading services. The numbers shown are the respective rarity numbers from the Universal Rarity Chart.

Classification is meant as a rough guide showing what is "typically" included in a "complete" set of Lincoln Cents. Common, Semi-Key, or Key designators refer to coins that are typically included; Sub-Varieties are not needed for a complete set. Remember to collect what you want: there is no right or wrong way to assemble a collection.

1909 reverse.

Weight: 3.11 grams
Diameter: 19 mm
Composition: .950 copper, .050 tin and zinc

🕒 **Timeline:** The Lincoln Cent is issued August 2, 1909.

1909

Mintage: 72,702,618
Mintage Rarity: R43
MSR: R17
Spectral Rarity: R17
Classification: Common

A few reverses show excessive tooling marks where the initials V.D.B. were filed off the master dies in Philadelphia.

1909 Doubled Rev. Die

Mintage: Inc. above
Mintage Rarity: –
MSR: R6
Spectral Rarity: R5
Classification: Sub-Variety

Two varieties similar to the following.

1909 VDB Doubled Obv. Die

Mintage: Inc. above
Mintage Rarity: –
MSR: R12
Spectral Rarity: R9
Classification: Sub-Variety

There are at least three minor doubling variations. The most sought after by error collectors has doubling most notably on the date, and somewhat on LIBERTY.

1909 Matte Proof

Mintage: 2,198
Mintage Rarity: R18
PR: R14
Spectral Rarity: R11
Classification: Key

Lincon Cents can have two types of finish. The most common is similar to the "Roman

The 1909 VDB Doubled Obverse Die (right and above right) has doubling most notably on the date and somewhat on LIBERTY.

Gold" finish, but some coins have a matte finish with pronounced grain. The majority of all matte proofs in this series are stained or streaked and have nice to dark toning because of the yellow paper they were shipped in from the mint. The details should be clean and sharp, notably Lincoln's beard and curls. The rims should be broad and flat with sharp inner and outer edges. A wire rim should be evident on the obverse and the reverse, unlike chamfered rims of a business strike. The edge should not be beveled with the rim, as this is a characteristic of a business strike. Authentication is highly recommended.

1909 VDB Matte Proof (left); close-up (right).

1909 VDB Matte Proof
Mintage: 420
Mintage Rarity: R14
PR: R10
Spectral Rarity: R7
Classification: Key

One die pair was used to manufacture all 420 specimens, so all have the same distinct characteristics. Die polish lines oriented roughly from eleven to five o'clock are just below and to the right of the tip of Lincoln's nose. On the reverse is a very small crescent-shaped die chip located to the right of the "M" of UNUM. The wire rim should have square corners and be fairly concentric around the coin's axis. The rim should be broad and flat with sharp inner and outer edges. A wire rim should be evident on the obverse and the reverse, unlike chamfered rims of a business strike. Authentication is highly recommended.

1909 VDB
Mintage: 27,995,000
Mintage Rarity: R41
MSR: R20
Spectral Rarity: R20
Classification: Common

Many of these coins are available in uncirculated grades because they were first year of issue. Full red specimens with full mint luster are

1909 VDB (cont.)

readily available. These coins are especially good for looking at the V.D.B. initials on the reverse. One or more of the periods may be faint or missing altogether. The initials are typically sharp at the top and grow faint toward the bottom.

1909S

Mintage: 1,825,000
Mintage Rarity: R35
MSR: R17
Spectral Rarity: R16
Classification: Key

There were six obverse dies used. One was also used to make the 1909S VDB variety (with mintmark in position number one). Die Number 3 has various stages of die deterioration, which is a result of using the die beyond its expected life. This makes the area around the mintmark look grainy, similar to those of the later years.

Below: Note the groove or notch in the right serif of the S mintmark on the 1909S VDB. There is also a die chip in the upper loop. Right: The 1909S VDB reverse.

1909S VDB

Mintage: 484,000
Mintage Rarity: R32
MSR: R19
Spectral Rarity: R16
Classification: Key

Undeniably the most well-known variety in all numismatics. Four working obverse dies were used to make the 1909S VDB. The same S mintmark was used on all Lincoln Cent production dies at the San Francisco Mint from 1909 to 1917. The mintmark should have parallel serifs with a groove or notch in the right serif. There is also a die chip in the upper loop.

Die No. 1 obverse.

Die No. 1: The S is close to the date, directly below the "90" in "1909," and the right side of the S lines up with the left curve of the "0." The S tilts to the right at a slight angle, and the top of the S is above the bottom of the nines in the date. On the field of the obverse a small raised piece of metal is evident, caused by a slight die chip located above the "0" and to the right of the top lip of Lincoln.

Die No. 2: The S is very similar to Die No. 1, but the angle at which it tilts to the right is not as great. The top of the S is even with the bottoms of the nines in the date. On later die state specimens, a slight raised line is evident above the "U" in TRUST. This was caused by the cavitation of the die, which was improperly heat treated.

Die No. 3: The top of the S is even with the bottoms of the nines in the date. The mintmark is slightly tilted to the right and the left edge of the S is even with the center spacing between the "9" and "0."

Die No. 2 obverse.

Die No. 3 obverse.

Die No. 4 obverse.

Die No. 4: The S is lower than on the other two dies and is more below the "0" in "1909." The S is also vertical, and the mintmark may appear to reside in a slight depression, with the left edge even with the left edge of "0." On the mating reverse die, the initials V.D.B. on the reverse may be faint, more so toward the bottom. On the "B" the bottom and center bars must slope downward diagonally to the left. This characteristic is common for all true VDB cents. Die No. 4 is the most common of the four varieties and is the most easily identified.

Collector's Tip: Be careful when purchasing one of these coins, as several counterfeits have been made. These are very deceptive, even to the most knowledgeable collector. Do not use the number of dots on the reverse as an indication of authenticity.

1909S Over Hor. S

Mintage: Inc. above
Mintage Rarity: –
MSR: R11
Spectral Rarity: R10
Classification: RPM Sub-Variety

The first mintmark is rotated clockwise to about the two o'clock position; the second mintmark is over it. The top loop and serif should be highly visible. Later coins from this die show less of the first S and are not typically collected by error specialists.

1909S/S

Mintage: Inc. above
Mintage Rarity: –
MSR: R5
Spectral Rarity: R2
Classification: RPM Sub-Variety

Not as common as the previous repunched mintmark variety.

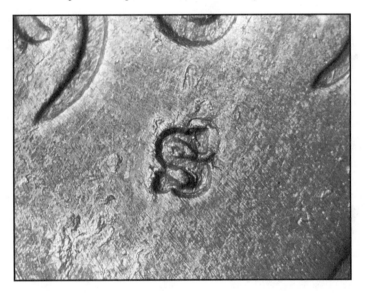

1910

Mintage: 146,801,218
Mintage Rarity: R45
MSR: R16
Spectral Rarity: R15
Classification: Common

1910 Matte Proof

Mintage: 2,405
Mintage Rarity: R19
PR: R14
Spectral Rarity: R10
Classification: Key

Proofs are often satin finish.

1910 Matte Proof (VDB)

Mintage: Inc. above
Mintage Rarity: –
MSR: R1
Spectral Rarity: –
Classification: Sub-Variety

Bill Fivaz, member of the Society of Lincoln Cent Collectors, was the first to discover the faint remains of Brenner's initials on a 1910 Matte Proof coin. It was common to use reverse dies as long as possible, even if they were used past the year of issue. Of the three known specimens (MS and Proof) part of the "D" and the majority of the "B" remain. The two lesser known specimens are from the San Francisco Mint. All three specimens were discovered by members of the Society of Lincoln Cent Collectors.

1910S

Mintage: 6,045,000
Mintage Rarity: R37
MSR: R17
Spectral Rarity: R15
Classification: Semi-Key

These coins were not hoarded like those of 1909, and thus are a lot more difficult to find in full mint red state. Exceptional uncirculated (MS65 and above) specimens are very scarce.

1911

Mintage: 101,177,787
Mintage Rarity: R44
MSR: R15
Spectral Rarity: R14
Classification: Common

1911 Matte Proof

Mintage: 1,733
Mintage Rarity: R18
PR: R13
Spectral Rarity: R8
Classification: Key

Similar to those of 1912 and 1913. Typically these coins have a very pronounced matte finish which is very grainy in appearance. This feature makes these proof coins difficult to detect and grade. Very difficult to locate full red uncirculated specimens.

1911D

Mintage: 12,672,000
Mintage Rarity: R39
MSR: R15
Spectral Rarity: R13
Classification: Semi-Key

Typically weakly struck. The same D mintmark was used from 1911 to 1917 and thus any one-cent coins struck at the Denver Mint will have the same mintmark characteristics. The serifs are clear and the opening or loop of the D is actually triangular in appearance.

1911S

Mintage: 4,026,000
Mintage Rarity: R37
MSR: R15
Spectral Rarity: R12
Classification: Semi-Key

Very difficult to locate full red uncirculated specimens.

1911S/S

Mintage: Inc. above
Mintage Rarity: –
MSR: R4
Spectral Rarity: R2
Classification: RPM Sub-Variety

1912

Mintage: 68,153,060
Mintage Rarity: R43
MSR: R15
Spectral Rarity: R13
Classification: Common

1912 Matte Proof

Mintage: 2,145
Mintage Rarity: R18
PR: R13
Spectral Rarity: R7
Classification: Key

See 1911 Matte Proof description.

1912D

Mintage: 10,411,000
Mintage Rarity: R39
MSR: R14
Spectral Rarity: R12
Classification: Semi-Key

Very difficult to locate full red uncirculated specimens.

1912S
Mintage: 4,431,000
Mintage Rarity: R37
MSR: R14
Spectral Rarity: R11
Classification: Semi-Key

Very difficult to locate full red uncirculated specimens.

1912S/S
Mintage: Inc. above
Mintage Rarity: –
MSR: R4
Spectral Rarity: –
Classification: RPM Sub-Variety

1913
Mintage: 76,532,352
Mintage Rarity: R43
MSR: R15
Spectral Rarity: R13
Classification: Common

1913 Matte Proof
Mintage: 2,848
Mintage Rarity: R19
PR: R14
Spectral Rarity: R11
Classification: Key

See 1910 Matte Proof description. The most obtainable of all the matte proofs. Again, be careful of uncirculated 1913 cents being passed off as proofs. Authentication is highly recommended.

1913D
Mintage: 15,804,000
Mintage Rarity: R40
MSR: R14
Spectral Rarity: R12
Classification: Semi-Key

1913S
Mintage: 6,101,000
Mintage Rarity: R37
MSR: R14
Spectral Rarity: R11
Classification: Semi-Key

Very difficult to locate full red uncirculated specimens.

1913S/S
Mintage: Inc. above
Mintage Rarity: –
MSR: R1
Spectral Rarity: –
Classification: RPM Sub-Variety

1914

Mintage: 75,238,432
Mintage Rarity: R43
MSR: R15
Spectral Rarity: R13
Classification: Common

1914 Matte Proof

Mintage: 1,365
Mintage Rarity: R17
PR: R13
Spectral Rarity: R9
Classification: Key

See description for 1911 Matte Proof.

1914D

Mintage: 1,193,000
Mintage Rarity: R34
MSR: R13
Spectral Rarity: R10
Classification: Key

A very elusive coin in fine uncirculated condition. Most often seen with red-brown toning. There were six obverse and seven reverse dies used in production that year for all 1.19 million coins struck. Several types of counterfeits exist, mostly in uncirculated grades. Look for added mintmarks to those coins struck in Philadelphia—the field will show buffing or polishing marks around the mintmark and the mintmark may appear to be a different color than the field. Easier to identify are counterfeits made from coins dated 1944. The position of

A true 1914D will often show the mintmark residing in a slight depression and will have the same characteristics as any cents made at the Denver Mint from 1911 to the middle of 1917.

Here is a counterfeit 1914D made from a 1944 cent. Counterfeits typically have a larger gap between the "9" and the "1."

the date on the coin is irrelevant, but all numerals should have equal spacing. Counterfeits typically have a larger gap between the nine and the one. Also look for the initials V.D.B. on the trunk of Lincoln: if these are present it is a counterfeit. These coins are typically weakly struck.

Collector's Tip: The key to authentication of this coin is the mintmark style. A true 1914D will often show the mintmark residing in a slight depression and will have the same characteristics as any cents made at the Denver Mint from 1911 to the middle of 1917. With six obverse dies, mintmark location can vary greatly and is of minimal use in authentication. Struck, transfer die counterfeits exist, but they can often be authenticated by the edges. Genuine cents generally have beveled edges; the counterfeits are squared or have proof-like edges as a result of the counterfeiter's effort to get the most detail from his die by increasing the striking pressure. Struck counterfeits also display lack of detail, low relief, toolmarks, and depressions. On lower grade specimens be careful of 1918D cents that were changed to look like a 1914D. There have been reports of a small hoard of approximately seven hundred uncirculated specimens that went undiscovered until the 1950s. However, I have been unable to prove or disprove this story.

1914S
Mintage: 4,137,000
Mintage Rarity: R37
MSR: R13
Spectral Rarity: R9
Classification: Semi-Key

Most often seen with Red-Brown or Brown toning.

1915
Mintage: 29,092,120
Mintage Rarity: R41
MSR: R15
Spectral Rarity: R13
Classification: Common

1915 Matte Proof
Mintage: 1,150
Mintage Rarity: R17
PR: R12
Spectral Rarity: R7
Classification: Key

Very difficult to locate full red uncirculated specimens.

1915D
Mintage: 22,050,000
Mintage Rarity: R40
MSR: R15
Spectral Rarity: R13
Classification: Common

Very difficult to locate full red uncirculated specimens.

1915S
Mintage: 4,833,000
Mintage Rarity: R37
MSR: R13
Spectral Rarity: R9
Classification: Semi-Key

Very difficult to locate full red uncirculated specimens.

🕒 **Timeline:** The obverse portrait of Lincoln is modified to extend die life. The portrait is made slightly smaller, with Lincoln's coat and cheek having less detail.

1916
Mintage: 131,833,677
Mintage Rarity: R45
MSR: R16
Spectral Rarity: R15
Classification: Common

1915 obverse.

1916 obverse.

1916 Matte Proof

Mintage: 1,050
Mintage Rarity: R17
PR: R11
Spectral Rarity: R6
Classification: Key

The most difficult of the matte proofs to authenticate.

1916D

Mintage: 35,956,000
Mintage Rarity: R42
MSR: R14
Spectral Rarity: R11
Classification: Common

1916S

Mintage: 22,510,000
Mintage Rarity: R40
MSR: R14
Spectral Rarity: R10
Classification: Semi-Key

Very difficult to locate full red uncirculated specimens.

1917

Mintage: 196,429,785
Mintage Rarity: R46
MSR: R15
Spectral Rarity: R14
Classification: Common

1917 Doubled Obv. Die

Mintage: Inc. above
Mintage Rarity: –
MSR: –
Spectral Rarity: –
Classification: Sub-Variety

Two varieties with doubling most obvious on the date.

1917 Matte Proof

Mintage: 500(?)
Mintage Rarity: R15(?)
PR: –
Spectral Rarity: –
Classification: Sub-Variety

These coins were illegally made, and the U.S. Mint denies ever making any proof one-cent coins in 1917. Authentication is recommended if you encounter a suspect specimen.

1917 Doubled Obverse Die.

1917 Matte Proof (cont.)

Collector's Tip: Be careful of first strike uncirculated specimens being passed off as proof versions.

1917D
Mintage: 55,120,000
Mintage Rarity: R43
MSR: R14
Spectral Rarity: R12
Classification: Common

Typically weakly struck.

1917S
Mintage: 32,620,000
Mintage Rarity: R41
MSR: R14
Spectral Rarity: R9
Classification: Semi-Key

Very difficult to locate full red uncirculated specimens.

Timeline: The initials of Victor David Brenner are restored to the truncation on the obverse a few months after the death of Charles Barber, chief opponent to Brenner and chief engraver of the Mint. The initials are placed there by George T. Morgan, most famous for the silver dollar bearing his name.

1918
Mintage: 288,104,634
Mintage Rarity: –
MSR: R15
Spectral Rarity: R13
Classification: Common

1918D
Mintage: 47,830,000
Mintage Rarity: R42
MSR: R14
Spectral Rarity: R11
Classification: Common

Typically weakly struck.

1918S
Mintage: 34,680,000
Mintage Rarity: R42
MSR: R13
Spectral Rarity: R9
Classification: Semi-Key

Often weakly struck. Uncirculated specimens with full red color are difficult to locate.

1919

Mintage: 392,021,000
Mintage Rarity: –
MSR: R16
Spectral Rarity: R16
Classification: Common

1919D

Mintage: 57,154,000
Mintage Rarity: R43
MSR: R14
Spectral Rarity: R12
Classification: Common

1919S

Mintage: 139,760,000
Mintage Rarity: R45
MSR: R14
Spectral Rarity: R10
Classification: Semi-Key

Very difficult to locate full red uncirculated specimens.

1920

Mintage: 310,165,000
Mintage Rarity: –
MSR: R16
Spectral Rarity: R15
Classification: Common

1920D

Mintage: 49,280,000
Mintage Rarity: R42
MSR: R14
Spectral Rarity: R12
Classification: Common

1920S

Mintage: 46,220,000
Mintage Rarity: R42
MSR: R13
Spectral Rarity: R9
Classification: Semi-Key

Difficult to find full red uncirculated specimens.

1921

Mintage: 39,157,000
Mintage Rarity: R42
MSR: R15
Spectral Rarity: R14
Classification: Common

Typically weakly struck.

1921S

Mintage: 15,274,000
Mintage Rarity: R40
MSR: R15
Spectral Rarity: R10
Classification: Semi-Key

Often weakly struck with lack of crisp detail. Difficult to find uncirculated specimens with full red color.

1922D

Mintage: 7,160,000
Mintage Rarity: R38
MSR: R15
Spectral Rarity: R13
Classification: Semi-Key

There were twenty obverse and twenty-seven reverse dies used to strike these coins from January through February.

1922D "No D" Obverse Dies Number 1 and 3 (Die Pairs #1 and #3)

Mintage: Inc. above
Mintage Rarity: –
MSR: R8

1922D obverse.

The 1922D "No D" Obverse Dies Number 1 and 3 variety has a very weak reverse with a lack of detail. The wheat ears are blurred or have no lines at all. It also has either a "jogging" or straight die crack running from the left half of the "L" in PLURIBUS through the "O" in ONE.

Spectral Rarity: R4
Classification: Sub-Variety

These rarities are the result of poor planning on behalf of the Mint. On February 26, the Denver Mint ran out of usable dies with approximately five hundred thousand Lincoln Cents to strike to fill its quota for the year. When asked to send replacement dies, Philadelphia said no new dies would be forthcoming. As a result, the obverse and reverse dies were well worn, and as the obverse dies struck coins, dirt and oil (also known as "mint grease") filled the incuse area of the mintmarks, which, depending on the amount accumulated, would produce "No D" or "Shadow D" cents. The "plug" of dirt and oil would fall out only to reform. This die pair is not exclusive of the "No D" variety. The mintmark should not be visible at all to the naked eye under normal lighting conditions.

This variety has a very weak reverse with a lack of detail. The wheat ears are blurred or have no lines at all. It also has either a "jogging" or straight die crack running from the left half of the "L" in PLURIBUS through the "O" in ONE. On the obverse, most detail would be comparable to a Very Good or Fine circulated specimen. The "R" in LIBERTY is blurred or flat looking and is joined with the "T." The "L" in LIBERTY runs into the rim and the lettering of IN GOD WE looks blurred. The first "T" in TRUST is more distinct and noticeably smaller than the second "T." The coat of Lincoln is faded toward his chest under the date and is weakly struck at the head, and the second "2" of 1922 is weaker than the first.

The American Numismatic Association Authentication Bureau has conducted studies that prove this process of progressive deterioration and die filling repeated itself several times. The mintmark faded in and out continuously as the dies became increasingly worn. In the past, determination of the status of 1922 cents struck from dies #1 and #3 has been an extremely subjective process.

A close-up of a jogging die crack found on the reverse of the 1922D "No D" Obverse Dies Number 1 and 3.

A close-up of a straight die crack found on the reverse of the 1922D "No D" Obverse Dies Number 1 and 3.

1922D "No D" Obverse Dies Number 1 and 3 (cont.)

Notice the blurring of the "R" in LIBER-TY and how the "L" runs into the rim on the 1922D "No D" Obverse Dies Number 1 and 3.

1922D "No D" Obverse Die Number 2 (Die Pair #2)

Mintage: Inc. above
Mintage Rarity: –
MSR: R7
Spectral Rarity: R3
Classification: Key

Die pair #2 evolved in a different manner. A pair of slightly worn dies producing normal 1922D cents clashed together, damaging the reverse die. The obverse die, though worn and marred by the die clash, still was considered usable. Apparently, the reverse die was extensively damaged, perhaps even shattered, and was discarded. The obverse die was removed from the press, reworked and polished, and matched with a new reverse die.

During reworking of the obverse die, sufficient metal was removed from the die face to erase all traces of the D mintmark. Consequently, every specimen struck from this second pair of dies is of the "No D" variety. No subjective judgment is required in determining this variety, as the diagnostics for this die are easily recognized. Another desirable feature of this variety is its superior eye appeal. Because these coins were struck from a slightly worn obverse die and a new reverse die, they exhibit fairly normal details. The second "2" in the date is sharper than the first, and the letters in TRUST are sharp. The letters of WE are only slightly blurred. This die pair is the only die pair of the "No D" variety recognized by the American Numismatic Association. The 1922D "No D" cent is exceedingly rare in uncirculated condition; in fact, it is the rarest in the entire series. Do not underestimate the rarity of this variety.

1923

Mintage: 74,723,000
Mintage Rarity: R43
MSR: R14
Spectral Rarity: R13
Classification: Common

Typically weakly struck.

1923S

Mintage: 8,700,000
Mintage Rarity: R38
MSR: R13
Spectral Rarity: R10
Classification: Semi-Key

Typically weakly struck, with full red uncirculated specimens being somewhat difficult to locate.

○ **Timeline:** Victor David Brenner dies at age fifty-three in New York City.

1924

Mintage: 75,178,000
Mintage Rarity: R43
MSR: R14
Spectral Rarity: R14
Classification: Common

Typically weakly struck.

1924D

Mintage: 2,520,000
Mintage Rarity: R36
MSR: R14
Spectral Rarity: R10
Classification: Key

Usually has a weak mintmark. In the past, there was an interest in a sub-variety that was referred to as the 1924D broken D cent, which showed a die break on the mintmark. This sub-variety was extensively marketed and publicized, but was too common to gain long-standing collector support. Most cents struck during this period were weakly struck due to improper hardening of the working dies.

1924S Type I

Mintage: 11,696,000
Mintage Rarity: R39
MSR: R13
Spectral Rarity: R9
Classification: Semi-Key

Often weakly struck. Difficult to find uncirculated specimens with full red color.

1924S Type II (Goiter Neck Variety)

Mintage: Inc. above
Mintage Rarity: –
MSR: –
Spectral Rarity: –
Classification: Sub-Variety

Typically weakly struck. Another sub-variety that was over publicized and lost the interest of collectors.

1925

Mintage: 139,949,000
Mintage Rarity: R45
MSR: R16
Spectral Rarity: R15
Classification: Common

1925D

Mintage: 22,580,000
Mintage Rarity: R40
MSR: R15
Spectral Rarity: R12
Classification: Common

Typically weakly struck. Difficult to locate full red uncirculated specimens.

1925S

Mintage: 26,380,000
Mintage Rarity: R41
MSR: R13
Spectral Rarity: R9
Classification: Semi-Key

See previous description.

1925S Doubled Obv. Die

Mintage: Inc. above
Mintage Rarity: –
MSR: R2
Spectral Rarity: –
Classification: Sub-Variety

1925S/S

Mintage: Inc. Above
Mintage Rarity: –
MSR: R3
Spectral Rarity: –
Classification: Sub-Variety

1926

Mintage: 157,088,000
Mintage Rarity: R45
MSR: R17
Spectral Rarity: R17
Classification: Common

Full red uncirculated specimens are abundant and should be easy to locate.

1926 Doubled Obv. Die

Mintage: Inc. above
Mintage Rarity: –
MSR: –
Spectral Rarity: –
Classification: Sub-Variety

A very minor doubled obverse die exists. Minor doubled dies are a fairly common occurrence from the 1920s through the late 1940s.

1926D
Mintage: 28,020,000
Mintage Rarity: R41
MSR: R14
Spectral Rarity: R11
Classification: Common

Full red uncirculated specimens are scarcer than for the Philadelphia issue.

1926S
Mintage: 4,550,000
Mintage Rarity: R37
MSR: R13
Spectral Rarity: R8
Classification: Key

Typically weakly struck. Full red uncirculated specimens are seemingly much scarcer for this variety than for the Philadelphia and Denver issues.

Collector's Tip: Be careful of coins that have been processed or dipped.

1927
Mintage: 144,440,000
Mintage Rarity: R45
MSR: R15
Spectral Rarity: R14
Classification: Common

1927 Doubled Obv. Die
Mintage: –
Mintage Rarity: –
MSR: R5
Spectral Rarity: R2
Classification: Sub-Variety

1927D
Mintage: 27,170,000
Mintage Rarity: R41
MSR: R14
Spectral Rarity: R12
Classification: Common

Typically weakly struck. Difficult to locate full red uncirculated specimens.

1927D/D
Mintage: Inc. above
Mintage Rarity: –
MSR: R2
Spectral Rarity: –
Classification: RPM Sub-Variety

1927S

Mintage: 14,276,000
Mintage Rarity: R39
MSR: R14
Spectral Rarity: R12
Classification: Semi-Key

Typically weakly struck.

1928

Mintage: 134,116,000
Mintage Rarity: R45
MSR: R15
Spectral Rarity: R15
Classification: Common

1928D

Mintage: 31,170,000
Mintage Rarity: R41
MSR: R14
Spectral Rarity: R12
Classification: Common

1928S Type I (Small S)

Mintage: 17,266,000
Mintage Rarity: R40
MSR: R13
Spectral Rarity: R11
Classification: Semi-Key

Typically weakly struck. Similarly to all previous cents from the San Francisco Mint, all are difficult to locate with full red color.

1928S Type II (Large S)

Mintage: Inc. above
Mintage Rarity: –
MSR: R4
Spectral Rarity: –
Classification: Sub-Variety

Mintmark has more defined serifs; several minor variations of repunched mintmarks. Typically weakly struck.

1929

Mintage: 185,262,000
Mintage Rarity: R46
MSR: R16
Spectral Rarity: R15
Classification: Common

1929 Doubled Obv. Die
Mintage: –
Mintage Rarity: –
MSR: –
Spectral Rarity: –
Classification: Sub-Variety

This variety shows only subtle hub doubling, mostly on the date.

1929D
Mintage: 41,730,000
Mintage Rarity: R42
MSR: R15
Spectral Rarity: R13
Classification: Common

Typically weakly struck.

1929S
Mintage: 50,148,000
Mintage Rarity: R42
MSR: R15
Spectral Rarity: R15
Classification: Common

Typically weakly struck.

1930
Mintage: 157,415,000
Mintage Rarity: R45
MSR: R18
Spectral Rarity: R18
Classification: Common

1930D
Mintage: 40,100,000
Mintage Rarity: R42
MSR: R16
Spectral Rarity: R15
Classification: Common

1930D Filled Zero
Mintage: –
Mintage Rarity: –
MSR: –
Spectral Rarity: –
Classification: Sub-Variety

1930S
Mintage: 24,286,000
Mintage Rarity: R41
MSR: R17
Spectral Rarity: R17
Classification: Common

Typically weakly struck.

1930S Doubled Obv. Die
Mintage: Inc. above
Mintage Rarity: –
MSR: –
Spectral Rarity: –
Classification: Sub-Variety

This is one of few early minor doubled die varieties from the San Francisco Mint.

1930S/S
Mintage: Inc. above
Mintage Rarity: –
MSR: R4
Spectral Rarity: R4
Classification: RPM Sub-Variety

1931
Mintage: 19,396,000
Mintage Rarity: R40
MSR: R15
Spectral Rarity: R15
Classification: Common

1931D
Mintage: 4,480,000
Mintage Rarity: R37
MSR: R16
Spectral Rarity: R12
Classification: Semi-Key

Full red uncirculated specimens are extremely difficult to obtain.

1931D/D
Mintage: Inc. above
Mintage Rarity: –
MSR: R1
Spectral Rarity: –
Classification: RPM Sub-Variety

1931S
Mintage: 866,000
Mintage Rarity: R33
MSR: R17
Spectral Rarity: R16
Classification: Key

Some specimens show an uneven strike. The Scharlack hoard contained over two hundred thousand (nearly one-quarter of all those minted) full red uncirculated specimens! This should be taken into consideration when looking at the rarity numbers.

Collector's Tip: Because this is a key in the series, be on the lookout for counterfeits. Most suspect coins have an S mintmark glued onto the field. Look closely at the seam where the mintmark touches the field; it should be a smooth transition with no voids, discolorations, or tooling marks. The easiest way to authenticate this type of fake is by using acetone to dissolve the glue. Another type of counterfeit is a 1936S made to look like a 1931S. On a real 1931S the last "1" in the date will be the same length as the first, and the top of the "3" should be rounded with the end curving sharply downwards. The bottom curve of the "3" is long and pointed and curves up next to the "9," differing greatly from the "3" on 1936S cents.

1932

Mintage: 9,062,000
Mintage Rarity: R38
MSR: R15
Spectral Rarity: R15
Classification: Common

1932D

Mintage: 10,500,000
Mintage Rarity: R39
MSR: R15
Spectral Rarity: R14
Classification: Semi-Key

1932D Doubled Obv. Die

Mintage: Inc. above
Mintage Rarity: –
MSR: R4
Spectral Rarity: R1
Classification: Sub-Variety

1933

Mintage: 14,360,000
Mintage Rarity: R39
MSR: R17
Spectral Rarity: R15
Classification: Common

1933D

Mintage: 6,200,000
Mintage Rarity: R37
MSR: R16
Spectral Rarity: R16
Classification: Common

1934

Mintage: 219,080,000
Mintage Rarity: R46
MSR: R15
Spectral Rarity: R5
Classification: Common

1934 Doubled Obv. Die

Mintage: –
Mintage Rarity: –
MSR: R3
Spectral Rarity: R3
Classification: Sub-Variety

1934D

Mintage: 28,446,000
Mintage Rarity: R41
MSR: R17
Spectral Rarity: R17
Classification: Common

1934D/D

Mintage: Inc. above
Mintage Rarity: –
MSR: R4
Spectral Rarity: R3
Classification: RPM Sub-Variety

There are at least two varieties of this repunched mintmark; both are very elusive.

1935

Mintage: 245,388,000
Mintage Rarity: R46
MSR: R15
Spectral Rarity: R15
Classification: Common

1935 Doubled Obv. Die

Mintage: Inc. above
Mintage Rarity: –
MSR: R5
Spectral Rarity: R4
Classification: Sub-Variety

At least two very minor varieties exist.

1935D

Mintage: 47,000,000
Mintage Rarity: R42
MSR: R15
Spectral Rarity: R14
Classification: Common

Typically weakly struck.

1935D/D
Mintage: Inc. above
Mintage Rarity: –
MSR: R1
Spectral Rarity: R1
Classification: RPM Sub-Variety

1935S
Mintage: 38,702,000
Mintage Rarity: R42
MSR: R15
Spectral Rarity: R14
Classification: Common

Typically weakly struck.

1935S/S
Mintage: Inc. above
Mintage Rarity: –
MSR: R1
Spectral Rarity: R1
Classification: RPM Sub-Variety

1936
Mintage: 309,637,569
Mintage Rarity: –
MSR: R15
Spectral Rarity: R15
Classification: Common

1936 Doubled Obv. Die
Mintage: Inc. above
Mintage Rarity: –
MSR: R10
Spectral Rarity: R9
Classification: Sub-Variety

The most common of the five varieties has doubling most visibly on the date and legends.

1936 Doubled Rev. Die
Mintage: Inc. above
Mintage Rarity: –
MSR: R5
Spectral Rarity: R1
Classification: Sub-Variety

1936 Doubled Obverse Die.

There are two varieties of the doubled reverse die. To date, a doubled obverse and doubled reverse on the same one-cent coin (less the '55 and '68 proof cents) has not been authenticated. A surprising number of dates in this series have both obverse and reverse doubled die varieties (mostly minor): 1936 through 1943 inclusively, 1946, 1955, 1957, 1959, 1962, 1963, 1964, 1972, and 1983.

1936 Proof Type I

Mintage: 3,700
Mintage Rarity: R20
PR: R12
Spectral Rarity: R10
Classification: Key

Proof cents made early in the year are less brilliant, with a satin type finish similar to uncirculated coins. A few coins were actually confused with business strikes and will show some evidence of wear.

1936 Proof Type II

Mintage: 1,869
Mintage Rarity: R18
PR: R15
Spectral Rarity: R15
Classification: Sub-Variety

These proof cents were made later in the year and have a more brilliant finish, similar to later years.

1936D

Mintage: 40,620,000
Mintage Rarity: R42
MSR: R15
Spectral Rarity: R15
Classification: Common

1936S

Mintage: 29,130,000
Mintage Rarity: R41
MSR: R14
Spectral Rarity: R14
Classification: Common

1937

Mintage: 309,179,320
Mintage Rarity: –
MSR: R16
Spectral Rarity: R16
Classification: Common

1937 Doubled Obv. Die

Mintage: Inc. above
Mintage Rarity: –
MSR: R5
Spectral Rarity: R5
Classification: Sub-Variety

At least three varieties exist. None are as common as the reverse doubled die.

1937 Doubled Rev. Die

Mintage: Inc. above
Mintage Rarity: –
MSR: R6
Spectral Rarity: R6
Classification: Sub-Variety

At least three varieties exist.

1937 Proof

Mintage: 9,320
Mintage Rarity: R22
PR: R16
Spectral Rarity: R16
Classification: Key

1937 Proof Doubled Rev. Die

Mintage: Inc. above
Mintage Rarity: –
MSR: R1
Spectral Rarity: R1
Classification: Sub-Variety

1937D

Mintage: 50,430,000
Mintage Rarity: R42
MSR: R16
Spectral Rarity: R16
Classification: Common

1937D Doubled Obv. Die

Mintage: Inc. above
Mintage Rarity: –
MSR: R6
Spectral Rarity: R6
Classification: Sub-Variety

Two varieties exist; one is more common than the other.

1937D/D

Mintage: Inc. above
Mintage Rarity: –
MSR: R6
Spectral Rarity: R6
Classification: RPM Sub-Variety

Three minor varieties exist.

1937S

Mintage: 34,500,000
Mintage Rarity: R41
MSR: R14
Spectral Rarity: R14
Classification: Common

1937S Doubled Obv. Die

Mintage: Inc. above
Mintage Rarity: –
MSR: R8
Spectral Rarity: R8
Classification: Sub-Variety

Two minor and one heavily doubled varieties exist.

1938

Mintage: 156,696,734
Mintage Rarity: R45
MSR: R14
Spectral Rarity: R12
Classification: Common

1938 Doubled Rev. Die

Mintage: Inc. above
Mintage Rarity: –
MSR: R4
Spectral Rarity: R4
Classification: Sub-Variety

Two varieties exist.

1938 Proof

Mintage: 14,734
Mintage Rarity: R23
PR: R17
Spectral Rarity: R16
Classification: Key

1938D

Mintage: 20,010,000
Mintage Rarity: R40
MSR: R15
Spectral Rarity: R15
Classification: Common

1938D/D

Mintage: Inc. above
Mintage Rarity: –
MSR: R8
Spectral Rarity: R7
Classification: RPM Sub-Variety

Three minor varieties exist.

1938D/D Doubled Rev. Die

Mintage: Inc. above
Mintage Rarity: –
MSR: R7
Spectral Rarity: R6
Classification: RPM Sub-Variety

Three varieties exist, and are attributed to the repunched mintmark and reverse die.

1938S

Mintage: 15,180,000
Mintage Rarity: R39
MSR: R12
Spectral Rarity: R12
Classification: Common

1938S Doubled Obv. Die

Mintage: Inc. above
Mintage Rarity: –
MSR: R2
Spectral Rarity: R1
Classification: Sub-Variety

Doubling not as visible as in the 1939 specimens.

1938S Doubled Rev. Die

Mintage: Inc. above
Mintage Rarity: –
MSR: R1
Spectral Rarity: R1
Classification: Sub-Variety

Only minor hub doubling is evident.

1938S/S

Mintage: Inc. above
Mintage Rarity: –
MSR: R10
Spectral Rarity: R10
Classification: RPM Sub-Variety

The most common, as well as popular, of all the 1938 varieties are the repunched mintmarks. Three varieties exist.

1938S/S/S

Mintage: Inc. above
Mintage Rarity: –
MSR: R11
Spectral Rarity: R11
Classification: RPM Sub-Variety

A very unique example of a triple repunched mintmark. A fairly easily obtainable coin in uncirculated condition. Other dates with triple repunched mintmarks include 1940S, 1945S, 1947S, 1950S, 1951D, 1952D, 1954D, 1955S, 1957D, 1958D, and 1959D.

The 1938S / S / S offers a very unique example of a triple repunched mintmark.

1939

Mintage: 316,479,520
Mintage Rarity: –
MSR: R15
Spectral Rarity: R15
Classification: Common

1939 Doubled Obv. Die

Mintage: Inc. above
Mintage Rarity: –
MSR: R5
Spectral Rarity: R2
Classification: Sub-Variety

Three varieties exist.

1939 Doubled Rev. Die

Mintage: Inc. above
Mintage Rarity: –
MSR: R2
Spectral Rarity: R2
Classification: Sub-Variety

1939 Proof Type I

Mintage: 13,520
Mintage Rarity: R23
PR: R17
Spectral Rarity: R16
Classification: Key

1939 Proof Type II

Mintage: Inc. above
Mintage Rarity: –
PR: R2
Spectral Rarity: R2
Classification: Sub-Variety

The second "9" in the date is noticeably smaller and thinner than the first. This was caused by excessive lapping of the die in preparation for striking proof coins. Not as common as Type I.

1939D

Mintage: 15,160,000
Mintage Rarity: R39
MSR: R15
Spectral Rarity: R15
Classification: Common

1939D/D

Mintage: Inc. above
Mintage Rarity: –
MSR: R8
Spectral Rarity: R8
Classification: RPM Sub-Variety

Three varieties exist; only one is easily visible.

1939S

Mintage: 52,070,000
Mintage Rarity: R43
MSR: R16
Spectral Rarity: R16
Classification: Common

1939S/S

Mintage: Inc. above
Mintage Rarity: –
MSR: R7
Spectral Rarity: R7
Classification: RPM Sub-Variety

Three varieties exist; only one is easily visible.

1940

Mintage: 586,825,872
Mintage Rarity: –
MSR: R13
Spectral Rarity: R13
Classification: Common

1940 Doubled Rev. Die

Mintage: Inc. above
Mintage Rarity: –
MSR: R6
Spectral Rarity: R6
Classification: Sub-Variety

Two minor varieties exist.

1940 Proof

Mintage: 15,872
Mintage Rarity: R23
PR: R16
Spectral Rarity: R16
Classification: Key

1940D

Mintage: 81,390,000
Mintage Rarity: R44
MSR: R14
Spectral Rarity: R14
Classification: Common

1940D/D

Mintage: Inc. above
Mintage Rarity: –
MSR: R4
Spectral Rarity: R4
Classification: RPM Sub-Variety

Four minor varieties exist.

1940S Type I (Large S, Plain 4)

Mintage: 112,940,000
Mintage Rarity: R44
MSR: R15
Spectral Rarity: R15
Classification: Common

1940S Type II (Small S, Crosslet 4)

Mintage: Inc. above
Mintage Rarity: –
MSR: –
Spectral Rarity: –
Classification: Sub-Variety

1940S Type III (Large S, Crosslet 4)

Mintage: Inc. above
Mintage Rarity: –
MSR: R5
Spectral Rarity: R5
Classification: Sub-Variety

The S mintmark is noticeably larger than those of previous years.

1940S Type IV (Large S over Small S, Crosslet 4)

Mintage: Inc. above
Mintage Rarity: –
MSR: –
Spectral Rarity: –
Classification: Sub-Variety

1940S Doubled Obv. Die

Mintage: Inc. above
Mintage Rarity: –
MSR: R4
Spectral Rarity: R3
Classification: Sub-Variety

1940S Doubled Rev. Die

Mintage: Inc. above
Mintage Rarity: –
MSR: R6
Spectral Rarity: R5
Classification: Sub-Variety

Two varieties exist.

1940S/S

Mintage: Inc. above
Mintage Rarity: –
MSR: R7
Spectral Rarity: R6
Classification: RPM Sub-Variety

Three varieties exist.

1940S/S/S

Mintage: Inc. above
Mintage Rarity: –
MSR: R6
Spectral Rarity: R6
Classification: RPM Sub-Variety

1941

Mintage: 887,039,100
Mintage Rarity: –
MSR: R14
Spectral Rarity: R14
Classification: Common

1941 Doubled Obv. Die

Mintage: Inc. above
Mintage Rarity: –
MSR: R9
Spectral Rarity: R8
Classification: Sub-Variety

Doubling most visible on LIBERTY and TRUST. There are at least five variations.

1941 Proof

Mintage: 21,100
Mintage Rarity: R24
PR: R16
Spectral Rarity: R16
Classification: Key

1941D
Mintage: 128,700,000
Mintage Rarity: R45
MSR: R16
Spectral Rarity: R16
Classification: Common

1941S Type I (Large S)
Mintage: 92,360,000
Mintage Rarity: R44
MSR: R15
Spectral Rarity: R15
Classification: Common

1941S Type II (Small S)
Mintage: Inc. above
Mintage Rarity: –
MSR: R6
Spectral Rarity: R6
Classification: Sub-Variety

Similar mintmark as in previous years.

1941S/S
Mintage: Inc. above
Mintage Rarity: –
MSR: R1
Spectral Rarity: R1
Classification: RPM Sub-Variety

1942
Mintage: 657,828,600
Mintage Rarity: –
MSR: R13
Spectral Rarity: R13
Classification: Common

1942 Doubled Obv. Die
Mintage: Inc. above
Mintage Rarity: –
MSR: R3
Spectral Rarity: R2
Classification: Common

At least three varieties exist.

1942 Proof
Mintage: 32,600
Mintage Rarity: R25
PR: R18
Spectral Rarity: R17
Classification: Key

1942D

Mintage: 206,698,000
Mintage Rarity: R46
MSR: R14
Spectral Rarity: R14
Classification: Common

1942D/D

Mintage: Inc. above
Mintage Rarity: –
MSR: R4
Spectral Rarity: R4
Classification: RPM Sub-Variety

At least three varieties exist.

1942S

Mintage: 85,590,000
Mintage Rarity: R44
MSR: R16
Spectral Rarity: R16
Classification: Common

1942S Doubled Obv. Die

Mintage: Inc. above
Mintage Rarity: –
MSR: R4
Spectral Rarity: R4
Classification: Sub-Variety

Doubling most visible on IN GOD WE TRUST and the "9" in the date. At least three varieties exist.

1942S/S Doubled Obv. Die

Mintage: Inc. above
Mintage Rarity: –
MSR: R6
Spectral Rarity: R6
Classification: DD-RPM Sub-Variety

Two distinct varieties exist.

1942S/S

Mintage: Inc. above
Mintage Rarity: –
MSR: R9
Spectral Rarity: R9
Classification: RPM Sub-Variety

At least five varieties exist. Only two varieties appear on the two doubled obverse die varieties.

Weight: 2.69 grams
Diameter: 19 mm
Composition: Steel, coated with zinc

Timeline: During World War II, copper—a previously almost worthless metal—is in short supply. Civilian matters are secondary to the military, so the shortage facing the Mint is not addressed until the problem becomes severe. Mint officials feel that Congress will eventually get around to the problem and certainly authorize a substitute for copper in the cent. The Mint sees no reason to delay their research, hoping to be able to start production with the new material as soon as the word is given. The logical alternatives to copper are tin, zinc, and nickel; however, these metals are also scarce, which is evidently why the Mint reduces the amount of tin in the cent from one percent to just a trace in 1941. In 1942 the Mint, desperate for any solution, goes to several private companies (Durez Plastics and Chemical Inc., and Colt's Firearms Company, just to name a few) to do testing for a substitute coinage material. It is at the Durez Plastics and Chemical Company that a small child of an employee is found playing with a new plastic cent. By 1943 that incident is publicized, and Mint Director Nellie Taylor Ross finally admits to the prototyping, which is not yet authorized by Congress.

In 1943 copper is required for the making of cartridge shells used during the war, and in an effort to ease the copper shortage, the Mint creates steel cents. The low carbon steel cents with a 0.0005-inch zinc coating are a disaster from the start. Because of the metals' inherent differences, they tend to corrode quickly. When first introduced, they are so disliked by the general population that they are often called "Steelies," "Lead Cents," or "Lead Pennies."

When the order is given for minting the steel cents on December 23, 1942, the official weight is to be 2.69 grams. Cents struck from February 23, 1942, until May 1943 are at the correct weight. Later, for unknown reasons, the Mint changes the weight of the cent to 2.75 grams, although the actual weight may fall within a very broad range.

The Mint begins to withdraw the steel cents from circulation in 1945. In the next twenty years, the Mint retrieves 163 million or 14.9% of the total minted. The Mint refuses to admit until 1959 that the cents are being withdrawn in fear that the coins will be hoarded.

For years, rumors keep resurfacing that the Ford Motor Company will give a new car to anyone who turns in a 1943 bronze cent. Although this rumor is denied and proven fraudulent, it persists even today.

1943

Mintage: 684,628,670
Mintage Rarity: –
MSR: R18
Spectral Rarity: –
Classification: Common

1943 Doubled Obv. Die

Mintage: Inc. above
Mintage Rarity: –
MSR: R4
Spectral Rarity: –
Classification: Sub-Variety

Two varieties exist.

1943 Doubled Rev. Die
Mintage: Inc. above
Mintage Rarity: –
MSR: R6
Spectral Rarity: –
Classification: Sub-Variety

Two varieties exist.

1943 Bronze
Mintage: 12(?)*
Mintage Rarity: R6(?)
MSR: –
Spectral Rarity: –
Classification: Sub-Variety

In 1943 a few planchets that were intended for 1942-dated bronze cents went unnoticed by Mint employees, either in the feed mechanisms or in hoppers, and were intermixed with the new steel planchets.

*At the time of this printing only twelve specimens have been authenticated.

Collector's Tip: Be careful if you come across a suspect specimen, as many forgeries have been made by plating regular steel cents with copper. True bronze varieties will be non-magnetic, will have the standard weight of 3.11 grams, and will have the tail of the "3" lower than the rest of the date. Alterations of the date are primarily focused on the 1948 Cent, which will have a different style of "3" than a 1943 Bronze or Steel Cent.
In 1965 the Mint Bureau released a press statement that the U.S. Mint never produced any 1943-dated bronze cents and that if any did exist they were counterfeit, even though one was owned by Mint engraver John R. Sinnock!

1943D
Mintage: 217,660,000
Mintage Rarity: R46
MSR: R19
Spectral Rarity: –
Classification: Common

1943D Doubled Obv. Die
Mintage: Inc. above
Mintage Rarity: –
MSR: R7
Spectral Rarity: –
Classification: Sub-Variety

1943D Doubled Rev. Die
Mintage: Inc. above
Mintage Rarity: –
MSR: R1
Spectral Rarity: –
Classification: Sub-Variety

1943D/D

Mintage: Inc. above
Mintage Rarity: –
MSR: R10
Spectral Rarity: –
Classification: RPM Sub-Variety

Seven varieties exist, with the most visible having the second D placed over half of the first D, but slightly lower and to the left.

1943D Bronze

Mintage: 6(?)
Mintage Rarity: R4(?)
MSR: –
Spectral Rarity: –
Classification: Sub-Variety

1943S

Mintage: 191,550,000
Mintage Rarity: R46
MSR: R18
Spectral Rarity: –
Classification: Common

1943S Doubled Obv. Die

Mintage: Inc. above
Mintage Rarity: –
MSR: R7
Spectral Rarity: –
Classification: Sub-Variety

Two minor varieties exist.

1943S Doubled Rev. Die

Mintage: Inc. above
Mintage Rarity: –
MSR: R6
Spectral Rarity: –
Classification: Sub-Variety

1943S obverse.

1943S/S

Mintage: Inc. above
Mintage Rarity: –
MSR: R3
Spectral Rarity: –
Classification: RPM Sub-Variety

1943S Bronze

Mintage: 6(?)
Mintage Rarity: R4(?)
MSR: –
Spectral Rarity: –
Classification: Sub-Variety

Weight: 3.11 grams
Diameter: 19 mm
Composition: .950 copper, .050 zinc.

🕒 **Timeline:** The year 1944 proves to be a milestone in cent production. It is the first time in the history of the United States that the Mint exceeds the one billion mark for any denomination, although today it would be considered a fairly small mintage.

Seventy percent copper, thirty percent zinc shell casings are intended to be used for actual coinage, but at the last moment enough copper becomes available to make brass cents rather than bronze cents. The cents from this period are often said to be made of "shell case bronze" mostly for patriotic reasons; it is highly doubtful that any shell casings are melted down to make cents other than for ceremonial reasons.

1944

Mintage: 1,435,400,00
Mintage Rarity: –
MSR: R14
Spectral Rarity: R13
Classification: Common

1944 Doubled Obv. Die

Mintage: Inc. above
Mintage Rarity: –
MSR: R6
Spectral Rarity: R6
Classification: Sub-Variety

Two varieties exist.

1944 Steel

Mintage: 15-20(?)
Mintage Rarity: R7(?)
MSR: R4
Spectral Rarity: –
Classification: Sub-Variety

These are rarer than their 1943 counterparts, but the process by which they came about is probably the same. The steel planchets went unnoticed in the feed mechanisms or hoppers and were intermixed and minted with regular 1944 planchets. They have typically weak details on high points of the design. John R. Sinnock also owned one of the 1944 Steel varieties.

1944D

Mintage: 430,578,000
Mintage Rarity: –
MSR: R13
Spectral Rarity: R13
Classification: Common

1944D Doubled Obv. Die

Mintage: Inc. above
Mintage Rarity: –
MSR: R5
Spectral Rarity: R4
Classification: Sub-Variety

Notice the top of the S is very visible above the D on the 1944D/S Type I. You should be able to see the S continue into the open loop of the D just below the top bar.

1944D/S Type I (Die #1)

Mintage: Inc. above
Mintage Rarity: –
MSR: R5
Spectral Rarity: R6
Classification: Semi-Key OMM Variety

This variety (Type I) is very elusive in any grade, especially in uncirculated Mint State. The top of the S is very visible above the D. The top of the S is above the bottom of the "9" in the date and the left edge of the S is very slightly to the left of the "4." You should be able to see the S continue into the open loop of the D just below the top bar.

1944D/S Type II (Die #2)

Mintage: Inc. above
Mintage Rarity: –
MSR: R11
Spectral Rarity: R10
Classification: Semi-Key OMM Variety

Type II is more common than Type I, yet it is more difficult to observe. The D was punched directly over the top of the S, almost obliterating it entirely. The curve of the S is just visible to the left of the bar in the D. Some raised metal inside and toward the bottom of the loop of the D

On the 1944D/S Type II, the D was punched directly over the top of the S, almost obliterating it entirely. The curve of the S is just visible to the left of the bar in the D.

is all that remains of the middle bar of the S, with a very minute portion of the bottom serif of the S visible directly below the tail of the D. The left side of the D mintmark should line up with the right side of the "9" in the date.

1944D/D
Mintage: Inc. above
Mintage Rarity: –
MSR: R7
Spectral Rarity: R7
Classification: RPM Sub-Variety

Four varieties exist.

1944S
Mintage: 282,760,000
Mintage Rarity: –
MSR: R13
Spectral Rarity: R13
Classification: Common

Most S mintmarks have blunt serifs but a few have sharp vertical serifs—the same mintmark as was used 1941-1943.

1944S/S
Mintage: Inc. above
Mintage Rarity: –
MSR: R2
Spectral Rarity: R2
Classification: RPM Sub-Variety

1945
Mintage: 1,040,515,000
Mintage Rarity: –
MSR: R11
Spectral Rarity: R11
Classification: Common

1945 Doubled Obv. Die
Mintage: Inc. above
Mintage Rarity: –
MSR: R4
Spectral Rarity: R4
Classification: Sub-Variety

1945D
Mintage: 266,268,000
Mintage Rarity: –
MSR: R12
Spectral Rarity: R12
Classification: Common

1945D Doubled Obv. Die
Mintage: Inc. above
Mintage Rarity: –
MSR: R9
Spectral Rarity: R9
Classification: Sub-Variety

Three varieties exist.

1945D/D
Mintage: Inc. above
Mintage Rarity: –
MSR: R4
Spectral Rarity: R4
Classification: Sub-Variety

Two varieties exist.

1945S
Mintage: 181,770,000
Mintage Rarity: R46
MSR: R14
Spectral Rarity: R14
Classification: Common

1945S/S
Mintage: Inc. above
Mintage Rarity: –
MSR: R3
Spectral Rarity: R2
Classification: RPM Sub-Variety

Two varieties exist.

1945S/S/S
Mintage: Inc. above
Mintage Rarity: –
MSR: R4
Spectral Rarity: R4
Classification: Sub-Variety

1946
Weight: 3.11 grams
Diameter: 19 mm
Composition: .950 copper, .050 tin and zinc

1946
Mintage: 991,655,000
Mintage Rarity: –
MSR: R10
Spectral Rarity: R10
Classification: Common

1946 Doubled Obv. Die
Mintage: Inc. above
Mintage Rarity: –
MSR: R3
Spectral Rarity: R3
Classification: Sub-Variety

1946 Doubled Rev. Die

Mintage: Inc. above
Mintage Rarity: –
MSR: R5
Spectral Rarity: R4
Classification: Sub-Variety

Two varieties exist, both showing only slight doubling.

1946D

Mintage: 315,690,000
Mintage Rarity: –
MSR: R11
Spectral Rarity: R11
Classification: Common

1946D/D

Mintage: Inc. above
Mintage Rarity: –
MSR: R7
Spectral Rarity: R7
Classification: RPM Sub-Variety

Five varieties exist.

1946S

Mintage: 198,100,000
Mintage Rarity: R46
MSR: R12
Spectral Rarity: R12
Classification: Common

A few specimens have an S mintmark with sharp vertical serifs. This was from an older punch, 1941-1943.

1946S Doubled Obv. Die

Mintage: Inc. above
Mintage Rarity: –
MSR: R4
Spectral Rarity: R4
Classification: Sub-Variety

Two varieties exist, showing only slight doubling.

1946S/D

Mintage: Inc. above
Mintage Rarity: –
MSR: R8
Spectral Rarity: R8
Classification: OMM Sub-Variety

This is an example of an overmintmark variety in which dies that were intended for use at the Denver Mint were actually used at the San Francisco Mint. This variety is not as popular as the 1944D/S.

1946S/S

Mintage: Inc. above
Mintage Rarity: –
MSR: R5
Spectral Rarity: R4
Classification: RPM Sub-Variety

Four varieties exist.

1947

Mintage: 190,555,000
Mintage Rarity: R46
MSR: R9
Spectral Rarity: R9
Classification: Common

1947 Doubled Obv. Die

Mintage: Inc. above
Mintage Rarity: –
MSR: R6
Spectral Rarity: R6
Classification: Sub-Variety

Two varieties exist, showing only slight doubling.

1947D

Mintage: 194,750,000
Mintage Rarity: R46
MSR: R11
Spectral Rarity: R11
Classification: Common

1947D/D

Mintage: Inc. above
Mintage Rarity: –
MSR: R4
Spectral Rarity: R4
Classification: RPM Sub-Variety

Two varieties exist.

1947S

Mintage: 99,000,000
Mintage Rarity: R44
MSR: R12
Spectral Rarity: R12
Classification: Common

Similar to previous years, a few specimens show the sharp vertical serifs from the older punch rather than the blunt serifs, which were more common.

1947S/S

Mintage: Inc. above
Mintage Rarity: –
MSR: R6
Spectral Rarity: R6
Classification: RPM Sub-Variety

Three varieties exist.

1947S/S/S

Mintage: Inc. above
Mintage Rarity: –
MSR: R1
Spectral Rarity: R1
Classification: RPM Sub-Variety

Very elusive compared to the S/S variety.

1948

Mintage: 317,570,000
Mintage Rarity: –
MSR: R10
Spectral Rarity: R10
Classification: Common

1948D

Mintage: 172,637,500
Mintage Rarity: R45
MSR: R9
Spectral Rarity: R9
Classification: Common

1948S

Mintage: 81,735,000
Mintage Rarity: R44
MSR: R11
Spectral Rarity: R11
Classification: Common

For some unknown reason, the S mintmark was changed back to the older style with straight vertical serifs rather than the blunt serifs. A few specimens have the blunt serifs.

1948S/S

Mintage: Inc. above
Mintage Rarity: –
MSR: R6
Spectral Rarity: R6
Classification: RPM Sub-Variety

1948S/S Doubled Obv. Die

Mintage: Inc. above
Mintage Rarity: –
MSR: R2
Spectral Rarity: R2
Classification: DD-RPM Sub-Variety

1949

Mintage: 217,775,000
Mintage Rarity: R46
MSR: R8
Spectral Rarity: R8
Classification: Common

1949D

Mintage: 153,132,500
Mintage Rarity: R45
MSR: R9
Spectral Rarity: R9
Classification: Common

1949D/D

Mintage: Inc. above
Mintage Rarity: –
MSR: R2
Spectral Rarity: R2
Classification: RPM Sub-Variety

Two varieties exist.

1949S

Mintage: 64,290,000
Mintage Rarity: R43
MSR: R11
Spectral Rarity: R11
Classification: Common

1949S Doubled Obv. Die

Mintage: Inc. above
Mintage Rarity: –
MSR: R4
Spectral Rarity: R4
Classification: Sub-Variety

Two varieties exist.

1949S/S

Mintage: Inc. above
Mintage Rarity: –
MSR: R8
Spectral Rarity: R8
Classification: RPM Sub-Variety

Three varieties exist.

1950
Mintage: 272,686,386
Mintage Rarity: –
MSR: R10
Spectral Rarity: R10
Classification: Common

1950 Proof
Mintage: 51,386
Mintage Rarity: R26
PR: R16
Spectral Rarity: R16
Classification: Key

Proof coinage resumed in 1950 after a lapse of eight years. The reintroduction of proof coins was delayed because the Philadelphia Mint was tied up for several years after World War II making medals that were awarded to veterans. Every man and woman who served during the war was entitled to a minimum of three medals. Early proofs are more satiny than those struck later, which are brilliant to date.

1950D
Mintage: 334,950,000
Mintage Rarity: –
MSR: R11
Spectral Rarity: R11
Classification: Common

1950S
Mintage: 118,505,000
Mintage Rarity: R45
MSR: R9
Spectral Rarity: R9
Classification: Common

1950S/S
Mintage: Inc. above
Mintage Rarity: –
MSR: R5
Spectral Rarity: R4
Classification: RPM Sub-Variety

Three varieties exist.

1950S/S/S
Mintage: Inc. above
Mintage Rarity: –
MSR: R2
Spectral Rarity: R2
Classification: RPM Sub-Variety

1951

Mintage: 284,633,500
Mintage Rarity: –
MSR: R7
Spectral Rarity: R7
Classification: Common

1951 Proof

Mintage: 57,500
Mintage Rarity: R26
PR: R15
Spectral Rarity: R15
Classification: Key

1951 Proof Doubled Obv. Die

Mintage: Inc. above
Mintage Rarity: –
PR: R8
Spectral Rarity: R8
Classification: Sub-Variety

1951 Proof Doubled Rev. Die

Mintage: Inc. above
Mintage Rarity: –
PR: –
Spectral Rarity: –
Classification: Sub-Variety

Very rare compared to the 1951 Doubled Obv. variety.

1951D

Mintage: 625,355,000
Mintage Rarity: –
MSR: R11
Spectral Rarity: R11
Classification: Common

1951D Doubled Obv. Die

Mintage: Inc. above
Mintage Rarity: –
MSR: R7
Spectral Rarity: R7
Classification: Sub-Variety

Three varieties exist.

1951D/D

Mintage: Inc. above
Mintage Rarity: –
MSR: R6
Spectral Rarity: R6
Classification: RPM Sub-Variety

Six varieties exist.

1951D/D/D

Mintage: Inc. above
Mintage Rarity: –
MSR: R1
Spectral Rarity: R1
Classification: RPM Sub-Variety

1951D/S

Mintage: Inc. above
Mintage Rarity: –
MSR: R8
Spectral Rarity: R8
Classification: OMM Sub-Variety

This overmintmark sub-variety has traces of the S in the loop of the D, visible only under extreme magnification.

1951S

Mintage: 136,010,000
Mintage Rarity: R45
MSR: R11
Spectral Rarity: R11
Classification: Common

1951S/S

Mintage: Inc. above
Mintage Rarity: –
MSR: R5
Spectral Rarity: R5
Classification: RPM Sub-Variety

Four varieties exist.

1952

Mintage: 186,856,980
Mintage Rarity: R46
MSR: R8
Spectral Rarity: R7
Classification: Common

1952 Proof

Mintage: 81,980
Mintage Rarity: R27
PR: R15
Spectral Rarity: R15
Classification: Key

1952D

Mintage: 746,130,000
Mintage Rarity: –
MSR: R11
Spectral Rarity: R11
Classification: Common

1952D/D

Mintage: Inc. above
Mintage Rarity: –
MSR: R6
Spectral Rarity: R6
Classification: RPM Sub-Variety

Four varieties exist.

1952D/S

Mintage: Inc. above
Mintage Rarity: –
MSR: R7
Spectral Rarity: R6
Classification: OMM Sub-Variety

There are two overmintmark variations. Both have only a trace of the S in the loop of the D, visible only under extreme magnification.

1952S

Mintage: 137,800,004
Mintage Rarity: R45
MSR: R8
Spectral Rarity: R8
Classification: Common

1952S/S

Mintage: Inc. above
Mintage Rarity: –
MSR: R4
Spectral Rarity: R4
Classification: RPM Sub-Variety

1953

Mintage: 256,883,800
Mintage Rarity: R46
MSR: R8
Spectral Rarity: R8
Classification: Common

The date has the same long-tailed three as was used in 1934 and 1943.

1953 Proof

Mintage: 128,800
Mintage Rarity: R28
PR: R15
Spectral Rarity: R15
Classification: Key

1953 Proof Doubled Obv. Die

Mintage: Inc. above
Mintage Rarity: –
PR: R10
Spectral Rarity: R10
Classification: Sub-Variety

At least three varieties exist.

1953D

Mintage: 700,515,000
Mintage Rarity: –
MSR: R9
Spectral Rarity: R9
Classification: Common

1953D/D (D over L)

Mintage: Inc. above
Mintage Rarity: –
MSR: R4
Spectral Rarity: R4
Classification: Sub-Variety

Four varieties exist, with the most visible having the first D punched at a sharp angle. The second D was punched over the top of the first with just the bar and the leg of the first D visible. Often incorrectly called a "D over L" variety because the remains of the first D look like the letter "L."

1953S

Mintage: 181,835,000
Mintage Rarity: R46
MSR: R8
Spectral Rarity: R8
Classification: Common

1953S/S

Mintage: Inc. above
Mintage Rarity: –
MSR: R8
Spectral Rarity: R8
Classification: RPM Sub-Variety
Six varieties exist.

1954

Mintage: 71,873,350
Mintage Rarity: R43
MSR: R10
Spectral Rarity: R9
Classification: Common

1954 Proof

Mintage: 233,300
Mintage Rarity: R30
PR: R15
Spectral Rarity: R15
Classification: Key

1954 Proof Doubled Rev. Die

Mintage: Inc. above
Mintage Rarity: –
PR: R3
Spectral Rarity: R3
Classification: Sub-Variety

1954D
Mintage: 251,552,500
Mintage Rarity: R46
MSR: R10
Spectral Rarity: R10
Classification: Common

1954D/D
Mintage: Inc. Above
Mintage Rarity: –
MSR: R2
Spectral Rarity: –
Classification: RPM Sub-Variety

1954D/D/D
Mintage: Inc. Above
Mintage Rarity: –
MSR: R1
Spectral Rarity: R1
Classification: RPM Sub-Variety

1954S
Mintage: 96,190,000
Mintage Rarity: R44
MSR: R11
Spectral Rarity: R11
Classification: Common

1954S Doubled Obv. Die
Mintage: Inc. above
Mintage Rarity: –
MSR: R5
Spectral Rarity: R5
Classification: Sub-Variety

Two varieties exist.

1954S/S
Mintage: Inc. above
Mintage Rarity: –
MSR: R6
Spectral Rarity: R6
Classification: RPM Sub-Variety

Five varieties exist, with only a trace of the original mintmark showing.

1954S "BIE"
Mintage: Inc. above
Mintage Rarity: –
MSR: R7
Spectral Rarity: R7
Classification: "BIE" Sub-Variety

A die break between the "B" and the "E" in the word LIBERTY resulted in what looks like the letter "I." To date, over eighteen hundred such varieties have been cataloged, with enough of a collector following to form a national organization, The "BIE" Guild. In this book I only list the most popular and commonly collected varieties, mostly from the 1950s and 1960s.

🕐 **Timeline:** The San Francisco Mint officially closes its doors and once again becomes known as the San Francisco Assay Office.

1955

Mintage: 330,958,200
Mintage Rarity: –
MSR: R10
Spectral Rarity: R10
Classification: Common

1955 "Poor Man's Double Die"

Mintage: Inc. above
Mintage Rarity: –
MSR: –
Spectral Rarity: –
Classification: Sub-Variety

This coin is as far from a doubled die as one can get. The doubling of the last "5," or sometimes both "5"s in the date, is actually caused by abrasion, not by the hubbing process. When the obverse die began to show wear, a mint employee polished the die, creating a faint step near the incuse portion of the date, thus creating the effect known as abrasion doubling.

1955 Doubled Obv. Die

Mintage: 20,000-24,000(?)
Mintage Rarity: R24
MSR: R16
Spectral Rarity: R11
Classification: Key

The 1955 Doubled Obverse Die is the most visible and well-known hub doubling example of the entire series, with doubling most visible on the date and the legends LIBERTY and IN GOD WE TRUST. The hair details are less sharp than what would be considered typical for cents of the period. The Mint knew that several thousand "error" coins were made, but rather than destroying the entire lot, Sydney C. Engel decided to release all ten million coins intermixed with the doubled die varieties in order to keep up with production schedules. These coins are very difficult to locate in uncirculated condition with full red mint luster and are typically found with Red-Brown color. This variety is fairly easy to authenticate from die markers on the one die pair used to produce it.

Collector's Tips: All known genuine 1955 Doubled Obverse Die cents display lines of die polish to the left of the upright in the "T" in CENT. A low level pinpoint light source placed at ninety degrees to this linear polish is recommended for easiest detection. Another little known characteristic is the stepped rim, which can be found at the twelve o'clock position toward the obverse.

1955 Doubled Obv. Die (cont.)

The 1955 Doubled Obverse Die is the most visible and well-known hub doubling example of the entire Lincoln Cent series, with doubling most visible on the date and the legends LIBERTY and IN GOD WE TRUST.

1955 Doubled Rev Die

Mintage: Inc. above
Mintage Rarity: –
MSR: R6
Spectral Rarity: R6
Classification: Sub-Variety

1955 Proof

Mintage: 378,200
Mintage Rarity: R31
PR: R15
Spectral Rarity: R15
Classification: Key

1955 Proof Doubled Obv. Die

Mintage: Inc. above
Mintage Rarity: –
PR: R6
Spectral Rarity: R6
Classification: Sub-Variety

Three varieties exist and are not as common as the following.

1955 Proof Doubled Rev. Die

Mintage: Inc. above
Mintage Rarity: –
PR: R10
Spectral Rarity: R10
Classification: Sub-Variety

Five varieties exist.

1955 Proof Doubled Obv. and Doubled Rev. Die

Mintage: Inc. above
Mintage Rarity: –
PR: R10
Spectral Rarity: R10
Classification: Sub-Variety

1955 was the definitely the year of the doubled dies. Two dates, 1955 and 1968, have two doubled dies on the same coin, and both happen to be fairly easily obtainable proofs.

1955D

Mintage: 563,257,500
Mintage Rarity: –
MSR: R11
Spectral Rarity: R9
Classification: Common

1955D/D

Mintage: Inc. above
Mintage Rarity: –
MSR: R6
Spectral Rarity: R6
Classification: RPM Sub-Variety

1955S

Mintage: 44,610,000
Mintage Rarity: R42
MSR: R12
Spectral Rarity: R11
Classification: Common

A gentleman by the name of Robert Friedberg managed to assemble a hoard of over seven million uncirculated 1955S cents. This should be taken into consideration when looking at the rarity numbers.

1955S "BIE"

Mintage: Inc. above
Mintage Rarity: –
MSR: R9
Spectral Rarity: R9
Classification: "BIE" Sub-Variety

1955S/S

Mintage: Inc. above
Mintage Rarity: –
MSR: R3
Spectral Rarity: R3
Classification: RPM Sub-Variety

Two varieties exist.

1955S/S/S

Mintage: Inc. above
Mintage Rarity: –
MSR: R7
Spectral Rarity: R7
Classification: RPM Sub-Variety

Two varieties exist.

1955S "Capped Head"

Mintage: Inc. above
Mintage Rarity: –
MSR: –
Spectral Rarity: –
Classification: Sub-Variety

An interesting variety that was caused when part of the reverse die broke off over the right wheat ear, resulting in a cud die break. The loose piece of die steel was struck between the dies, denting the obverse die on Lincoln's head. This variety is also referred to as the "cracked skull" variety.

1956

Mintage: 421,414,384
Mintage Rarity: –
MSR: R7
Spectral Rarity: R6
Classification: Common

1956 Proof

Mintage: 669,384
Mintage Rarity: R33
PR: R13
Spectral Rarity: R13
Classification: Key

1956 Proof Doubled Obv. Die

Mintage: Inc. above
Mintage Rarity: –
PR: R9
Spectral Rarity: R9
Classification: Sub-Variety

Six varieties exist.

1956 Proof Doubled Rev. Die

Mintage: Inc. above
Mintage Rarity: –
PR: R7
Spectral Rarity: R7
Classification: Sub-Variety

Three varieties exist.

1956D

Mintage: 1,098,210,100
Mintage Rarity: –
MSR: R8
Spectral Rarity: R7
Classification: Common

1956D/D

Mintage: Inc. above
Mintage Rarity: –
MSR: R11
Spectral Rarity: R11
Classification: RPM Sub-Variety

Of the five varieties, the one most visible has the first mintmark placed too low. The die was repaired and the second mintmark is found in typical location. Remains of the first mintmark are slightly visible; the first D is below and completely separate from the second D. This is one of the more common RPM varieties, easily found with full red luster.

🕐 **Timeline:** The Prudential Insurance Company "invests" in one hundred thousand proof sets at the time of issue. Although this is less than ten percent of the total mintage, it is enough of a hoard to drop the bottom out for 1957 proof sets. The sets sell for $2.10 from the Mint and in a few short months are being sold for only $1.60.

1957

Mintage: 283,787,952
Mintage Rarity: –
MSR: R7
Spectral Rarity: R6
Classification: Common

1957 Proof

Mintage: 1,247,952
Mintage Rarity: R34
PR: R13
Spectral Rarity: R13
Classification: Key

1957 Proof Doubled Rev. Die

Mintage: Inc. above
Mintage Rarity: –
PR: R6
Spectral Rarity: R6
Classification: Sub-Variety

Two varieties exist.

1957D

Mintage: 1,051,342,000
Mintage Rarity: –
MSR: R8
Spectral Rarity: R7
Classification: Common

1957D Doubled Obv. Die

Mintage: Inc. above
Mintage Rarity: –
MSR: R7
Spectral Rarity: R7
Classification: Sub-Variety

   Two varieties exist.

1957D/D Doubled Obv. Die

Mintage: Inc. above
Mintage Rarity: –
MSR: R9
Spectral Rarity: R9
Classification: DD-RPM Sub-Variety

   Six varieties exist.

1957D/D

Mintage: Inc. above
Mintage Rarity: –
MSR: R3
Spectral Rarity: R3
Classification: RPM Sub-Variety

1957D/D/D

Mintage: Inc. above
Mintage Rarity: –
MSR: R4
Spectral Rarity: R4
Classification: RPM Sub-Variety

   Two varieties exist.

1958

Mintage: 253,400,652
Mintage Rarity: R46
MSR: R9
Spectral Rarity: R8
Classification: Common

1958 Doubled Obv. Die

Mintage: Inc. above
Mintage Rarity: –
MSR: –
Spectral Rarity: –
Classification: Sub-Variety

   A minor doubled die with doubling most visible on the words LIBERTY and IN GOD WE TRUST.

1958/7

Mintage: Inc. above
Mintage Rarity: –
MSR: R11
Spectral Rarity: R11
Classification: OD Sub-Variety

If this variety is genuinely an overdate, it is one of the most bizarre coins in the entire series. If it is genuine, a mint employee used a 1957 working hub (used to make working dies) to create a 1958 master die (used to make working hubs). The "7" was almost completely effaced by polishing the area and an "8" was added to the new master die. The remains of the supposed "7" are clearly visible only under extreme magnification (30X+). The most visible on all varieties is the point of the bar of the "7" on the upper-right-hand side of the "8."

Many collectors feel that it is simply a die gouge that looks similar to the bar of a "7." I am not thoroughly convinced that this is simply a die gouge. The area of the loop adjoining the "die gouge" shows no evidence of abrasion or tooling and the size and location are indicative of the size and location of the bar of the "7" on 1957 cents. However, a Very Early Die State specimen has not been submitted to the American Numismatic Association Authentication Bureau for examination under an electron microscope for authentication and surface mapping.

The validity of this variety will be hotly debated until a more thorough investigation has been conducted and more conclusive proof is found.

1958 Proof

Mintage: 875,652
Mintage Rarity: R33
PR: R13
Spectral Rarity: R13
Classification: Key

1958 Proof Doubled Rev. Die

Mintage: Inc. above
Mintage Rarity: –
PR: R3
Spectral Rarity: R3
Classification: Sub-Variety

Two varieties exist.

1958D

Mintage: 800,953,300
Mintage Rarity: –
MSR: R8
Spectral Rarity: R8
Classification: Common

1958/7D

Mintage: Inc. above
Mintage Rarity: –
MSR: R12
Spectral Rarity: R12
Classification: OD Sub-Variety

See description for 1958/7 sub-variety. The 1958/7D variety is more common than the 1958/7 variety.

1958/7 D/D

Mintage: Inc. above
Mintage Rarity: –
MSR: R8
Spectral Rarity: R8
Classification: OD RPM Sub-Variety

Two varieties exist, showing evidence of repunched mintmarks, including one with a horizontal D to the left of the normal mintmark.

1958D/D/D

Mintage: Inc. above
Mintage Rarity: –
MSR: R4
Spectral Rarity: R4
Classification: RPM Sub-Variety

🕐 **Timeline:** The U.S. Mint holds an internal contest among the staff engravers at the Philadelphia Mint for a new reverse for the Lincoln Cent. A total of twenty-three designs are submitted by three engravers, with the design of Frank Gasparro, an assistant engraver (later promoted to chief engraver) at the Mint, winning hands down. Although Frank Gasparro never visits the Lincoln Memorial before he creates the new reverse, the splendor and accuracy of the building is impressive.

The construction of the Lincoln Memorial in Washington D.C. was begun on February 12, 1915, and dedicated on Memorial Day, 1922. The memorial design is by Henry Bacon and features thirty-six columns that taper inward toward the top of the structure to prevent it from looking too top heavy. These columns represent the number of states in the union at the time of Lincoln's term in office. The nineteen-foot-high statue of the seated emancipator was created by Daniel Chester French and is highly detailed on the reverse of the new cent. Ironically, Gasparro was born in Philadelphia in 1909, the year the Lincoln Cent was created, and the one hundredth anniversary of Lincoln's birth. Gasparro studied at the Pennsylvania Academy of Fine Arts and the Fleisher Art Memorial and joined the Mint in 1942.

The design for the new reverse is chosen by Treasury Secretary Anderson and Mint Director W. H. Brett, and is presented to the Lincoln Sesquicentennial Committee. The contest for the new design is not open to the public—in fact, the new reverse comes as quite a shock to many collectors who happen to discover it in circulation. The new cent goes into production on January 2, and is first released to the public on February 12, 1959—the 150th anniversary of the birth of Abraham Lincoln.

The new Lincoln Cent is one of only two coins minted with the same person on the obverse and the reverse. The first was the Commemorative Lafayette dollar of 1900 with Lafayette appearing on both sides of the coin.

1959

Mintage: 610,864,291
Mintage Rarity: –
MSR: R7
Spectral Rarity: R6
Classification: Common

1959 Doubled Obv. Die

Mintage: Inc. above
Mintage Rarity: –
MSR: R6
Spectral Rarity: R6
Classification: Sub-Variety

Three varieties exist.

1959 Doubled Rev. Die

Mintage: Inc. above
Mintage Rarity: –
MSR: R4
Spectral Rarity: R4
Classification: Sub-Variety

Two varieties exist.

1959 Proof

Mintage: 1,149,291
Mintage Rarity: R34
PR: R13
Spectral Rarity: R13
Classification: Key

1959 Proof Doubled Rev. Die

Mintage: Inc. above
Mintage Rarity: –
PR: R4
Spectral Rarity: R4
Classification: Sub-Variety

Two varieties exist.

1959D

Mintage: 1,279,760,000
Mintage Rarity: –
MSR: R6
Spectral Rarity: R6
Classification: Common

1959D/D

Mintage: Inc. above
Mintage Rarity: –
MSR: R4
Spectral Rarity: R4
Classification: RPM Sub-Variety

Three varieties exist, showing only microscopic traces of the original mintmark.

1959D/D/D

Mintage: Inc. above
Mintage Rarity: –
MSR: R9
Spectral Rarity: R9
Classification: RPM Sub-Variety

Four varieties exist.

In 1959 the Lincoln Cent was released with a new reverse. Shown on the top is the old reverse; shown on the bottom is the new reverse featuring the impressive Lincoln Memorial. The new Lincoln Cent is one of only two coins minted with the same person on the obverse and the reverse.

1960 (Large Date)

Mintage: 588,096,602
Mintage Rarity: –
MSR: R6
Spectral Rarity: R6
Classification: Common

The large date variety can be determined by the large tail of the "6," and the top of the "1" being below the top of the "9." The numerals themselves are thinner than the small date variety. The date was slightly enlarged because the incuse date on the die tended to fill up with oil, debris, and so on, resulting in a weaker image.

1960 (Large Date) Doubled Rev. Die

Mintage: Inc. above
Mintage Rarity: –
MSR: R3
Spectral Rarity: R3
Classification: Sub-Variety

Two varieties exist; both are very rare.

1960 (Small Date)

Mintage: –
Mintage Rarity: –
MSR: R9
Spectral Rarity: R9
Classification: Common

The small date variety can be determined by the smaller tail of the "6," and the top of the "1" being below the top of the "9."

1960 Proof (Large Date)

Mintage: 1,691,602
Mintage Rarity: R35
PR: R13
Spectral Rarity: R13
Classification: Key

See description for 1960 Large Date.

1960 Proof (Large Date) Doubled Obv. and Rev. Die

Mintage: Inc. above
Mintage Rarity: –
PR: R1
Spectral Rarity: R1
Classification: Sub-Variety

A very rare and unique variety.

1960 Proof (Large Date) Doubled Rev. Die

Mintage: Inc. above
Mintage Rarity: –
PR: R7
Spectral Rarity: R7
Classification: Sub-Variety

1960 Proof (Large Date/Small Date)
Mintage: Inc. above
Mintage Rarity: –
PR: R10
Spectral Rarity: R10
Classification: Sub-Variety

Four varieties exist.

1960 Proof (Small Date)
Mintage: Inc. above
Mintage Rarity: –
PR: R15
Spectral Rarity: R15
Classification: Key

See description for 1960 Small Date.

1960 Proof (Small Date) Doubled Obv. Die
Mintage: Inc. above
Mintage Rarity: –
PR: R4
Spectral Rarity: R4
Classification: Sub-Variety

Two varieties exist.

1960 Proof (Small Date/Large Date)
Mintage: Inc. above
Mintage Rarity: –
PR: R10
Spectral Rarity: R10
Classification: Sub-Variety

Four varieties exist.

1960D (Large Date)
Mintage: 1,580,884,000
Mintage Rarity: –
MSR: R8
Spectral Rarity: R8
Classification: Common

See description for 1960 Large Date.

1960D Doubled Obv. Die (Large Date)
Mintage: Inc. above
Mintage Rarity: –
MSR: R7
Spectral Rarity: R7
Classification: Sub-Variety

Three varieties exist, showing only microscopic doubling. All three are very difficult to find.

The large date variety can be determined by the large tail of the "6" and the top of the "1" being below the top of the "9." The numerals themselves are thinner than the small date variety.

1960D/D (Large Date)
Mintage: Inc. above
Mintage Rarity: –
MSR: R8
Spectral Rarity: R8
Classification: RPM Sub-Variety

Twelve varieties exist, none as common as the 1960D/D Small Date/Large Date variety.

1960D/Lazy D (Large Date)
Mintage: Inc. above
Mintage Rarity: –
MSR: R3
Spectral Rarity: R3
Classification: RPM Sub-Variety

1960D/Horiz. D (Large Date)
Mintage: Inc. above
Mintage Rarity: –
MSR: R8
Spectral Rarity: R8
Classification: RPM Sub-Variety

Notice the doubling of the mintmark on the 1960D / D Large Date variety.

A fairly common and easily obtainable minting variety.

1960D (Small Date)
Mintage: Inc. above
Mintage Rarity: –
MSR: R8
Spectral Rarity: R7
Classification: Common

See description for 1960 Small Date.

1960D/D (Small Date)
Mintage: Inc. above
Mintage Rarity: –
MSR: R5
Spectral Rarity: R5
Classification: RPM Sub-Variety

1960D/D
(Small Date over Large Date)
Mintage: Inc. above
Mintage Rarity: –
MSR: R10
Spectral Rarity: R10
Classification: Sub-Variety

A very unique coin. The working die was hubbed first with a large date working hub, then with a small date working hub. This error

The small date variety can be determined by the smaller tail of the "6" and the top of the "1" being below the top of the "9."

is most visible on the "6" and the "0." The tail of the small "6" is clearly evident over the longer tail of the large "6." The "0" looks like a doughnut and the "9" shows clear evidence of the first "9" on its leg. The first D was punched very closely to the "9," above the main D, which is tilted about twenty degrees to the right.

A close-up of the 1960D small date variety.

The tail of the small "6" is clearly evident over the longer tail of the large "6" on the 1960D/D (Small Date over Large Date).

1961

Mintage: 756,373,244
Mintage Rarity: –
MSR: R5
Spectral Rarity: R5
Classification: Common

1961 Proof

Mintage: 3,028,244
Mintage Rarity: R36
PR: R14
Spectral Rarity: R12
Classification: Key

1961 Proof Doubled Obv. Die

Mintage: Inc. above
Mintage Rarity: –
PR: R6
Spectral Rarity: R6
Classification: Sub-Variety

Two varieties exist.

1961 Proof Doubled Obv. and Rev. Die

Mintage: Inc. above
Mintage Rarity: –
PR: R1
Spectral Rarity: R1
Classification: Sub-Variety

1961 Proof Doubled Rev. Die

Mintage: Inc. above
Mintage Rarity: –
PR: R4
Spectral Rarity: R4
Classification: Sub-Variety

1961D

Mintage: 1,753,266,700
Mintage Rarity: –
MSR: R5
Spectral Rarity: R5
Classification: Common

1961D/D

Mintage: Inc. above
Mintage Rarity: –
MSR: R8
Spectral Rarity: R8
Classification: RPM Sub-Variety

Eight varieties exist. These differ from the 1961D/Horiz. D and D/Lazy D varieties, as these are less noticeable and the mintmarks are more vertical in orientation.

1961D/D obverse.

1961D/Lazy D

Mintage: Inc. above
Mintage Rarity: –
MSR: R8
Spectral Rarity: R8
Classification: RPM Sub-Variety

The first D angles slightly to the left; the second D is almost vertical. The first D can be seen most clearly on the left side of the bar on the second D and inside its loop.

1961D/Horiz D

Mintage: Inc. above
Mintage Rarity: –
MSR: R11
Spectral Rarity: R11
Classification: RPM Sub-Variety

The first D is angled sharply to the left; the second D is almost vertical. This is the most common of all of the 1961 RPM varieties.

🕐 **Timeline:** The content of tin is reduced to levels similar to 1944-1946, essentially changing our bronze cents to brass.

1962

Mintage: 609,263,019
Mintage Rarity: –
MSR: R4
Spectral Rarity: R4
Classification: Common

1962 Doubled Obv. Die

Mintage: Inc. above
Mintage Rarity: –
MSR: R5
Spectral Rarity: R5
Classification: Sub-Variety

Four varieties exist.

1962 Doubled Rev. Die

Mintage: Inc. above
Mintage Rarity: –
MSR: R4
Spectral Rarity: R4
Classification: Sub-Variety

Three varieties exist.

1962 Proof

Mintage: 3,218,019
Mintage Rarity: R36
PR: R15
Spectral Rarity: R15
Classification: Key

1962

1962 Proof Doubled Obv. Die
Mintage: Inc. above
Mintage Rarity: –
PR: R8
Spectral Rarity: R8
Classification: Sub-Variety

1962 Proof Doubled Rev. Die
Mintage: Inc. above
Mintage Rarity: –
PR: R2
Spectral Rarity: R2
Classification: Sub-Variety

1962D
Mintage: 1,793,148,400
Mintage Rarity: –
MSR: R4
Spectral Rarity: R4
Classification: Common

1962 D/D
Mintage: Inc. above
Mintage Rarity: –
MSR: R1
Spectral Rarity: R1
Classification: RPM Sub-Variety

1963
Mintage: 757,185,645
Mintage Rarity: –
MSR: R4
Spectral Rarity: R4
Classification: Common

1963 Doubled Rev. Die
Mintage: Inc. above
Mintage Rarity: –
MSR: R4
Spectral Rarity: R4
Classification: Sub-Variety

Two varieties exist, showing only slight doubling under high magnification.

1963 Proof
Mintage: 3,075,645
Mintage Rarity: R36
PR: R15
Spectral Rarity: R15
Classification: Key

1963 Proof Doubled Obv. Die

Mintage: Inc. above
Mintage Rarity: –
PR: R2
Spectral Rarity: R2
Classification: Sub-Variety

1963 Proof Doubled Rev. Die

Mintage: Inc. above
Mintage Rarity: –
PR: R8
Spectral Rarity: R8
Classification: Sub-Variety

Five varieties exist.

1963D

Mintage: 1,774,020,400
Mintage Rarity: –
MSR: R6
Spectral Rarity: R6
Classification: Common

1963D Doubled Obv. Die

Mintage: Inc. above
Mintage Rarity: –
MSR: R8
Spectral Rarity: R8
Classification: Sub-Variety

A minor CCW rotated hub doubling variety most visible on the "3" in the date. Also referred to as a 1963/3D. Three similar varieties exist.

1963D Tripled Obv. Die

Mintage: Inc. above
Mintage Rarity: –
MSR: R6
Spectral Rarity: R6
Classification: Sub-Variety

A very unique example of rotated hub doubling showing three distinctly rotated impressions. The angle of rotation between each impression is very slight and the first impression is almost effaced by the other two impressions.

1963D/D

Mintage: Inc. above
Mintage Rarity: –
MSR: R1
Spectral Rarity: R1
Classification: RPM Sub-Variety

🕐 **Timeline:** Senator Bible of Nevada submits a bill to outlaw coin collecting in America as a way of easing the coinage shortage. Thankfully the bill does not pass.

1964

Mintage: 2,652,525,762
Mintage Rarity: –
MSR: R7
Spectral Rarity: R6
Classification: Common

1964 Doubled Obv. Die

Mintage: Inc. above
Mintage Rarity: –
MSR: R2
Spectral Rarity: R2
Classification: Sub-Variety

Two varieties exist. Not as common as the doubled reverse.

1964 Doubled Rev. Die

Mintage: Inc. above
Mintage Rarity: –
MSR: R11
Spectral Rarity: R11
Classification: Sub-Variety

At least ten varieties exist, all showing only slight hub doubling.

1964 Proof

Mintage: 3,950,762
Mintage Rarity: R37
PR: R16
Spectral Rarity: R16
Classification: Key

1964 Proof Doubled Rev. Die

Mintage: Inc. above
Mintage Rarity: –
PR: R8
Spectral Rarity: R8
Classification: Sub-Variety

Five varieties exist.

1964D

Mintage: 3,799,071,500
Mintage Rarity: –
MSR: R8
Spectral Rarity: R7
Classification: Common

This 1964 Doubled Reverse Die shows doubling most obvious on STATES OF.

🕒 **Timeline:** Mintmarks are outlawed to prevent hoarding of low mintage coins.

1965

Mintage: 1,497,224,900
Mintage Rarity: –
MSR: R8
Spectral Rarity: R8
Classification: Common

1965 (Special Mint Set)

Mintage: 2,360,000*
Mintage Rarity: R36
MSR: R10
Spectral Rarity: R10
Classification: Common

The Coinage Act of 1965 outlawed the use of mintmarks supposedly to prevent hoarding of coins with low mintage from any given mint. This law lasted on the books until the mintmarks were restored in 1968. With great deliberation, the Mint decided to restore the mintmark only as a way of determining the origin of mistakes on coins that were already released to the public so they could prevent those mistakes in the future.

As a way of pacifying and still making a profit off of collectors, the Mint created what was deemed a "Special Mint Set." These sets replaced proof sets from 1965 through 1967. The coins in these sets are rarely any better than typical uncirculated specimens that are available in "Mint Sets" offered by the Mint. A few possess proof-like qualities, but these are only from Very Early Die State strikes.

*Less the 62,000 unsold sets as reported by the Mint.

1966

Mintage: 2,188,147,783
Mintage Rarity: –
MSR: R5
Spectral Rarity: R4
Classification: Common

1966 (Special Mint Set)

Mintage: 2,261,583*
Mintage Rarity: R35
MSR: R11
Spectral Rarity: R11
Classification: Common

*Less the 114,000 unsold sets as reported by the Mint.

1967

Mintage: 3,048,667,100
Mintage Rarity: –
MSR: R4
Spectral Rarity: R4
Classification: Common

1967 (Special Mint Set)

Mintage: 1,863,344*
Mintage Rarity: R35
MSR: R11
Spectral Rarity: R11
Classification: Common

*Less the 27,000 unsold sets as reported by the Mint.

🕐 **Timeline:** At its discretion, the Mint decides to restore mintmarks after being illegal for three years. Proof coins are now made at the San Francisco branch rather than in Philadelphia.

1968

Mintage: 1,707,880,970
Mintage Rarity: –
MSR: R5
Spectral Rarity: R4
Classification: Common

1968 Doubled Obv. Die

Mintage: Inc. above
Mintage Rarity: –
MSR: R1
Spectral Rarity: R1
Classification: Sub-Variety

Very minor doubling visible only under extreme magnification.

1968D

Mintage: 2,886,269,600
Mintage Rarity: –
MSR: R6
Spectral Rarity: R6
Classification: Common

1968D/D

Mintage: Inc. above
Mintage Rarity: –
MSR: R1
Spectral Rarity: R1
Classification: RPM Sub-Variety

1968S

Mintage: 261,311,507
Mintage Rarity: R46
MSR: R7
Spectral Rarity: R6
Classification: Common

1968S Doubled Obv. Die

Mintage: Inc. above
Mintage Rarity: –
MSR: R1
Spectral Rarity: R1
Classification: Sub-Variety

Similar to the 1968 Doubled Obv. Die, minor doubling is visible only under extreme magnification.

1968S Proof

Mintage: 3,041,506
Mintage Rarity: R36
PR: R13
Spectral Rarity: R13
Classification: Key

1968S Proof Doubled Obv. Die

Mintage: Inc. above
Mintage Rarity: –
PR: R9
Spectral Rarity: R9
Classification: Sub-Variety

Six varieties exist.

1968S Proof Doubled Obv. and Rev. Die

Mintage: Inc. above
Mintage Rarity: –
PR: R2
Spectral Rarity: R2
Classification: Sub-Variety

🕐 **Timeline:** The U.S. Mint creates a new master die based on Brenner's original design of 1909. Over the years, the design on the old master die had spread out and had lost much of its detail through constant use.

The increased production of Lincoln Cents is the reason for building a new mint in Philadelphia this same year. Originally, there is to be but a single press designed by General Motors. Dubbed the "Coin Roller," it punches out, upsets, and strikes thousands of coins per minute, outpacing the older presses by leaps and bounds. The gargantuan "Coin Roller" contains a large rotating drum on which are mounted several dies that come into contact with the strip and complete the entire coin in one operation. The dies cannot handle the intense heat and pressure, however, and they fail prematurely. Because of this and the tediously long set-up time, the "Coin Roller" proves impractical for coinage production.

1969

Mintage: 1,136,910,000
Mintage Rarity: –
MSR: R4
Spectral Rarity: R4
Classification: Common

In 1969 the U.S. Mint created a new master die based on Brenner's original design of 1909. Notice the poor detailing on the 1968 coin (left) and the crisp detailing on the 1969 coin (right). Over the years, the design on the old master die had spread out and lost much of its detail through constant use.

1969 Doubled Obv. Die
Mintage: Inc. above
Mintage Rarity: –
MSR: R1
Spectral Rarity: R1
Classification: Sub-Variety

1969D
Mintage: 4,002,832,200
Mintage Rarity: –
MSR: R4
Spectral Rarity: R3
Classification: Common

1969D/D
Mintage: Inc. above
Mintage Rarity: –
MSR: R1
Spectral Rarity: R1
Classification: RPM Sub-Variety

1969S
Mintage: 547,309,631
Mintage Rarity: –
MSR: R10
Spectral Rarity: R10
Classification: Common

1969S Doubled Obv. Die

Mintage: Inc. above
Mintage Rarity: –
MSR: R4
Spectral Rarity: R2
Classification: Sub-Variety

This is one of the more recent doubled die varieties, with doubling most visible on the date. As always, be careful of machine doubling being passed off as a true doubled die variety.

1969S Proof

Mintage: 2,934,631
Mintage Rarity: R36
PR: R13
Spectral Rarity: R13
Classification: Key

1969S Doubled Obverse Die.

1970

Mintage: 1,898,315,000
Mintage Rarity: –
MSR: R6
Spectral Rarity: R6
Classification: Common

1970 Doubled Obv. Die

Mintage: Inc. above
Mintage Rarity: –
MSR: R4
Spectral Rarity: R4
Classification: Sub-Variety

1970D

Mintage: 2,891,438,900
Mintage Rarity: –
MSR: R6
Spectral Rarity: R6
Classification: Common

1970D Doubled Obv. Die

Mintage: Inc. above
Mintage Rarity: –
MSR: R6
Spectral Rarity: R6
Classification: Sub-Variety

Four varieties exist.

1970S (Large Date)

Mintage: 693,192,814
Mintage Rarity: –
MSR: R10
Spectral Rarity: R9
Classification: Common

The easiest way to distinguish between a large and small date variety is to look at the "9" and the "7" in the date. The small or level "7" variety has the loop of the "9" bent sharply toward the base of the "9"; the top of the "7" is even with the top of the "9," and the "7" will have a straight edge on the left-hand side of the stem. The large or low "7" variety will have the loop of the "9" angled about forty-five degrees and the top of the "7" will be lower than the top of the "9."

1970S Doubled Obv. Die (Large Date)

Mintage: Inc. above
Mintage Rarity: –
MSR: R7
Spectral Rarity: R7
Classification: Sub-Variety

At least six varieties exist. Doubling is most visible on the date, especially the "7" and the "0." Also known as the 1970/70 Doubled Obv. Die.

1970S/S (Large Date)

Mintage: Inc. above
Mintage Rarity: –
MSR: R9
Spectral Rarity: R9
Classification: RPM Sub-Variety

1970S (Small Date)

Mintage: Inc. above
Mintage Rarity: –
MSR: R13
Spectral Rarity: R13
Classification: Common

See description for 1970S Large Date.

1970S/S (Small Date)

Mintage: Inc. above
Mintage Rarity: –
MSR: R1
Spectral Rarity: R1
Classification: RPM Sub-Variety

1970S "Atheist Cent"

Mintage: Inc. above
Mintage Rarity: –
MSR: –
Spectral Rarity: –
Classification: Sub-Variety

The easiest way to distinguish between a large and small date 1970S is to look at the "9" and the "7" in the date. The small date variety shown above has the loop of the "9" bent sharply toward the base of the "9," and the top of the "7" is even with the top of the "9." The "7" has a straight edge on the left-hand side of the stem. In the large date variety the loop of the "9" is angled about 45 degrees and the top of the "7" is lower than the top of the "9."

The Lincoln Cent was the first one-cent denomination coin to carry the motto IN GOD WE TRUST, courtesy of then-president Taft, who refused to approve the coin's design without it. In 1970 at the San Francisco Mint, part of the obverse die broke away and the words WE TRUST were replaced by a cud, or a raised portion of metal, leaving only the words IN GOD at the top of the coin. A dealer with keen marketing skills quickly promoted this variety as the "Atheist Cent."

1970S Proof (Large Date)
Mintage: 2,632,810
Mintage Rarity: R36
PR: R13
Spectral Rarity: R13
Classification: Key

See description for 1970S Large Date.

1970S Proof (Large Date) Doubled Obv. Die
Mintage: Inc. above
Mintage Rarity: –
PR: R9
Spectral Rarity: –
Classification: Sub-Variety

Five varieties exist.

1970S Proof (Large Date) Tripled Obv. Die
Mintage: Inc. above
Mintage Rarity: –
PR: R6
Spectral Rarity: R6
Classification: Sub-Variety

1970S/S Proof (Large Date)
Mintage: Inc. above
Mintage Rarity: –
PR: R3
Spectral Rarity: R3
Classification: RPM Sub-Variety

1970S Proof (Small Date)
Mintage: Inc. above
Mintage Rarity: –
PR: R13
Spectral Rarity: R13
Classification: Key

See description for 1970S Large Date.

1970S Proof (Small Date) Doubled Obv. Die
Mintage: Inc. above
Mintage Rarity: –
PR: R8
Spectral Rarity: R7
Classification: Sub-Variety

1970S Proof (Small Date).

1971

Mintage: 1,919,490,000
Mintage Rarity: –
MSR: R5
Spectral Rarity: R5
Classification: Common

1971 Doubled Obv. Die

Mintage: Inc. above
Mintage Rarity: –
MSR: R11
Spectral Rarity: R8
Classification: Sub-Variety

Six varieties exist.

1971D

Mintage: 2,911,045,600
Mintage Rarity: –
MSR: –
Spectral Rarity: –
Classification: Common

1971S

Mintage: 528,354,192
Mintage Rarity: –
MSR: R6
Spectral Rarity: R6
Classification: Common

1971S Proof

Mintage: 3,220,733
Mintage Rarity: R36
PR: R10
Spectral Rarity: R10
Classification: Key

1971S Proof Doubled Obv. Die

Mintage: Inc. above
Mintage Rarity: –
PR: R10
Spectral Rarity: R10
Classification: Sub-Variety

The doubling on the 1971S Proof Doubled Obverse Die is most visible in GOD.

A rare doubled die proof variety that shows doubling plainest in LIBERTY and IN GOD WE TRUST. The doubling is most visible in GOD than in the other letters. Five varieties exist—all similar.

1971S/S

Mintage: Inc. above
Mintage Rarity: –
PR: R4
Spectral Rarity: R4
Classification: RPM Sub-Variety

1972

Mintage: 2,933,255,000
Mintage Rarity: –
MSR: R8
Spectral Rarity: R8
Classification: Common

1972 Doubled Obv. Die

Mintage: Inc. above
Mintage Rarity: –
MSR: R18
Spectral Rarity: R16
Classification: Key

A classic CW axial rotation doubling in which the die was slightly rotated between "impressions." Doubling is most visible on the words IN GOD WE TRUST and "LIBE" of LIBERTY. Only one die pair was used to create this variety. All known genuine specimens display a diagonal line of polish between the "IT" of UNITED on the reverse.

Doubling is most visible on the words IN GOD WE TRUST and "LIBE" of LIBERTY.

1972 Doubled Rev. Die

Mintage: Inc. above
Mintage Rarity: –
MSR: R6
Spectral Rarity: R6
Classification: Sub-Variety

Very rare compared to the 1972 Doubled Obverse varieties.

1972D

Mintage: 2,665,071,400
Mintage Rarity: –
MSR: R8
Spectral Rarity: R8
Classification: Common

1972D Doubled Obv. Die

Mintage: Inc. above
Mintage Rarity: –
MSR: R6
Spectral Rarity: R6
Classification: Sub-Variety

Five varieties exist. Doubling is not as visible as on the 1972 Doubled Obverse varieties.

1972D/D

Mintage: Inc. above
Mintage Rarity: –
MSR: R1
Spectral Rarity: R1
Classification: RPM Sub-Variety

1972D (No VDB)

Mintage: Inc. above
Mintage Rarity: –
MSR: R6
Spectral Rarity: R6
Classification: Sub-Variety

This variety seems to be rarer than similar occurrences in 1988, 1989, and 1990. This variety commands only a slight premium, and only in uncirculated condition, as the initials can easily be removed.

1972S

Mintage: 380,200,104
Mintage Rarity: –
MSR: R5
Spectral Rarity: R5
Classification: Key

1972S Proof

Mintage: 3,260,996
Mintage Rarity: R36
PR: R9
Spectral Rarity: R9
Classification: Key

1972S Proof Doubled Obv. Die

Mintage: Inc. above
Mintage Rarity: –
PR: R7
Spectral Rarity: R7
Classification: Sub-Variety

Four varieties exist.

◷ **Timeline:** The reverse dies are modified and the initials of Frank Gasparro (FG) are made larger.

1973

Mintage: 3,728,245,000
Mintage Rarity: –
MSR: R7
Spectral Rarity: R6
Classification: Common

1973D
Mintage: 3,549,576,588
Mintage Rarity: –
MSR: R7
Spectral Rarity: R6
Classification: Common

1973S
Mintage: 319,937,634
Mintage Rarity: –
MSR: R6
Spectral Rarity: R5
Classification: Common

1973S Proof
Mintage: 2,760,339
Mintage Rarity: R36
PR: R9
Spectral Rarity: R9
Classification: Key

🕒 **Timeline:** The reverse dies are modified yet again. The initials FG are made slightly smaller, but are still larger than pre-1973 cents. In November, the Mint begins making cents at the West Point Depository. Due to political and economical reasons, West Point is never deemed a "Branch" Mint, rather a depository for the Philadelphia Mint; thus, coins made there carry no mintmark and the quantities of cents minted there are jointly reported with those minted in Philadelphia.

1974
Mintage: 4,232,140,523
Mintage Rarity: –
MSR: R6
Spectral Rarity: R6
Classification: Common

1974D
Mintage: 4,235,098,000
Mintage Rarity: –
MSR: R7
Spectral Rarity: R7
Classification: Common

1974S
Mintage: 412,039,228
Mintage Rarity: –
MSR: R5
Spectral Rarity: R4
Classification: Common

1974S Proof
Mintage: 2,612,568
Mintage Rarity: R36
PR: R8
Spectral Rarity: R8
Classification: Key

1974S/S Proof
Mintage: Inc. above
Mintage Rarity: –
PR: R7
Spectral Rarity: R7
Classification: RPM Sub-Variety

1974 Pattern Aluminum Cent
Mintage: 1,579,324*
Mintage Rarity: R35
MSR: –
Spectral Rarity: –
Classification: –

*All but nine coins of the entire mintage were destroyed. One resides in The Smithsonian Institution's collection; the whereabouts of the others is unknown.

In 1973 the Arabian oil embargo, striking copper miners in Chile, the war in Zambia (both major copper producing countries), and the energy crisis had a critical effect on the price of copper on the world commodities market. If the price of copper rose above $1.28 per pound, the U.S. Mint would be losing money on the production of one-cent coins. The price of copper began to rise in early 1973, and it escalated from around $0.50 per pound to over $1.00 per pound in less than a year. The public was aware of the escalating price of copper and many parts of the country had shortages of one-cent coins as people began to hoard cents, hoping to realize a profit by so doing. Advertisements in non-numismatic publications compounded the problem, for example, by offering a roll (fifty coins) of one-cent coins for $1.50 each. Still others told unwary readers that copper cents dated 1974 would make great investments because they might be the last copper coins the Mint would produce.

Withdrawal of one-cent coins from the Federal Reserve system rose two hundred percent almost overnight. On April 18, 1974, the Secretary of the Treasury had to place a ban on the melting or exporting of one-cent coins. With no end of this trend in sight, the Secretary decided that a possible alternative metal for the one-cent coin was needed.

In July of 1973, the Secretary of the Treasury appointed Dr. Alan Goldman to initiate and head a study to find an acceptable replacement metal for the one-cent coin. At great expense, the Mint created nonsense dies that were designed to simulate the actual cent dies with regards to relief and location of the legends and devices. By doing so, the coining characteristics of other metals could be compared without creating a large number of potentially valuable numismatic oddities. Mint Director Mary T. Brooks was very aware of the potential security problems that could arise with the production of prototype coinage. A coining press was brought into the research and development laboratory to more closely monitor the number of coins being produced. Tests such as the accelerated wear-corrosion tests, which could not be performed within the confines of the lab, were performed elsewhere in the Mint using planchets.

The criteria used for evaluating new materials included the long-term supply and cost of raw material, the ease of coining, public acceptance, durability while in circulation, and the effect the new coin would have on existing coin-operated vending machines. The Mint looked at several possible replacement materials including copper-zinc alloys, aluminum alloys, bronze clad steel, aluminum clad steel, cupronickel clad zinc, and even stainless steel clad aluminum.

Of all the possible materials and alloys, the Mint decided to expend most of its time and resources investigating aluminum alloys. To establish a foundation for their research, the Mint looked at several European coins that were made of aluminum. The Mint determined that it could produce about 500 cents per pound of aluminum, compared to approximately 150 bronze cents per pound of copper. The greatest advantage of the aluminum over the other proposed alloys was the ease of fabricating it into strips and coins, and the current price of only $0.30 per pound. Cents made of aluminum would only cost the Mint six-hundredths of a cent in raw material—a vast improvement in seigniorage over the existing bronze cent. This would save the Mint over forty million dollars per year on metal costs alone. The Mint would also receive an additional savings of eight million kilowatt hours of electricity because the aluminum alloys did not need to be annealed before coining.

One-cent coins account for approximately seventy-five percent of the Mint's coin production, and about sixty-five percent of the raw materials used by the Mint each year. The Mint produces in excess of thirty million one-cent coins every operating day. With such a high production rate, the material to be chosen for the cent was very critical. The material had to be available at acceptable costs for a minimum of fifteen years. The price of bauxite ore, the raw material for aluminum, had been very stable on the futures market for a number of years and because of regional abundance, it was deemed that its price would not escalate in the foreseeable future. The Mint wanted to make sure that the new coin would not become a desirable source of expensive raw material.

Three aluminum alloys were considered for future study: alloys 1100 (commercially pure aluminum), 3003, and 5052. The latter two contained magnesium to improve hardness and resist wear. Alloys 1100 and 3003 were the most desirable because they required only low temperature annealing before being blanked. Alloy 5052 required only low temperature annealing to soften the metal prior to being coined to decrease the coining forces required. A minor problem arose when trying to coin alloy 1100—finning, or the appearance of a wire rim caused by metal extruding between the die and the collar, was observed. This was caused by the alloy's relative softness. It was the softest of the three alloys being tested and was immediately eliminated from further consideration. Alloys 3003 and 5052 did not show finning when coined on regular production dies dated 1974.

Between July and December 1973, the Mint produced 1,579,324 aluminum alloy 3003 (96.8% minimum aluminum, 1.2 % manganese) cents dated 1974 using actual production dies. During the run-off procedure it was determined that because of the new coin's low weight (.93 grams), the speed of the coining presses may have to be decreased from 120-130 strokes per minute to 110-120 strokes. Although the coining speeds may have had to be reduced, the die life for the new 3003 cent would far exceed the six hundred thousand strikes per die pair for the bronze cent because the coining forces were much lower.

Even with the proven coining methods and increased seigniorage to the Mint, the new aluminum cent was not to be. The Subcommittee on Consumer Affairs (of the Committee on Banking and Currency) squelched the cent based on testimony given by the vending machine lobby that said the new coin would jam their existing equipment. Additional testimony came from a doctor from Johns Hopkins University who stated that the new coin would not be visible on an x-ray if a child happened to swallow one. The Subcommittee did approve a measure that would allow the Mint at its discretion to change the composition of the bronze cent if the need arose. This authorization expired on December 31, 1977.

1975

Mintage: 5,451,476,142
Mintage Rarity: –
MSR: R5
Spectral Rarity: R5
Classification: Common

1975D

Mintage: 4,505,275,300
Mintage Rarity: –
MSR: R6
Spectral Rarity: R6
Classification: Common

1975S Proof

Mintage: 2,845,450
Mintage Rarity: R36
PR: R9
Spectral Rarity: R9
Classification: Key

1975S/S Proof

Mintage: Inc. above
Mintage Rarity: –
PR: R4
Spectral Rarity: R4
Classification: RPM Sub-Variety

1976

Mintage: 4,674,292,426
Mintage Rarity: –
MSR: R5
Spectral Rarity: R3
Classification: Common

1976 Doubled Obv. Die

Mintage: Inc. above
Mintage Rarity: –
MSR: R2
Spectral Rarity: R2
Classification: Sub-Variety

Two varieties exist, both exhibiting only minor hub doubling.

1976D

Mintage: 4,221,592,455
Mintage Rarity: –
MSR: R4
Spectral Rarity: R4
Classification: Common

1976S Proof
Mintage: 4,149,730
Mintage Rarity: R37
PR: R9
Spectral Rarity: R8
Classification: Key

1977
Mintage: 4,469,930,000
Mintage Rarity: –
MSR: R5
Spectral Rarity: R3
Classification: Common

1977D
Mintage: 4,194,062,300
Mintage Rarity: –
MSR: R4
Spectral Rarity: R4
Classification: Common

1977S Proof
Mintage: 3,251,152
Mintage Rarity: R36
PR: R9
Spectral Rarity: R9
Classification: Key

1978
Mintage: 5,558,605,000
Mintage Rarity: –
MSR: R6
Spectral Rarity: R4
Classification: Common

1978D
Mintage: 4,280,233,400
Mintage Rarity: –
MSR: R4
Spectral Rarity: R4
Classification: Common

1978S Proof
Mintage: 3,127,781
Mintage Rarity: R36
PR: R8
Spectral Rarity: R8
Classification: Key

1979

Mintage: 6,018,515,000
Mintage Rarity: –
MSR: R4
Spectral Rarity: R4
Classification: Common

1979D

Mintage: 4,139,357,254
Mintage Rarity: –
MSR: R3
Spectral Rarity: R3
Classification: Common

Several specimens exist without the initials FG on the reverse. This is a common phenomenon with the Lincoln Memorial cents—the initials in the die fill up with dirt, oil, and debris, or are obliterated by polishing the die to extend its life. The absence of the initials FG, or even VDB, on the reverse command only a slight premium, and then only on uncirculated coins.

1979S Proof Type I (Filled S)

Mintage: 2,848,175*
Mintage Rarity: R36
PR: R8
Spectral Rarity: R8
Classification: Key

Type I has a strong ridge on the mintmark from the top to lower serif with sharp ends on the serifs. Between the loops are raised areas of metal—hence the "Filled S" variety. Because the punch broke before finishing all of the proof dies, the Mint had to make a new punch, which did not match exactly.

*Mintage minus the official Mint estimate of Type II proof cents.

1979S Proof Type II (Clear S)

Mintage: 829,000*
Mintage Rarity: R33
PR: R11
Spectral Rarity: R11
Classification: Key Sub-Variety

Type II has a flattened mintmark with very rounded serifs. The serifs almost touch the middle bar.

*Official Mint estimate of mintage for Type II proof cents.

1980

Mintage: 7,414,705,000
Mintage Rarity: –
MSR: R6
Spectral Rarity: R6
Classification: Common

1980 Doubled Obv. Die
Mintage: 7,414,705,000
Mintage Rarity: –
MSR: R8
Spectral Rarity: R7
Classification: Sub-Variety

The doubling is most visible on the date, with overlapping openings in "80."

1980D
Mintage: 5,140,098,660
Mintage Rarity: –
MSR: R7
Spectral Rarity: R6
Classification: Common

1980D/S
Mintage: Inc. above
Mintage Rarity: –
MSR: R1
Spectral Rarity: R1
Classification: OMM Sub-Variety

Only a microscopic trace of the S remains in the field of the coin directly above the D mintmark.

1980S Proof
Mintage: 3,554,806
Mintage Rarity: R37
PR: R9
Spectral Rarity: R9
Classification: Key

1981
Mintage: 7,491,750,000
Mintage Rarity: –
MSR: R6
Spectral Rarity: R5
Classification: Common

1981D
Mintage: 5,373,235,677
Mintage Rarity: –
MSR: R7
Spectral Rarity: R6
Classification: Common

1981D/S
Mintage: Inc. above
Mintage Rarity: –
MSR: –
Spectral Rarity: –
Classification: Common

Similar to the 1980D over S variety.

1981S Proof Type I (Filled S)
Mintage: 3,464,083*
Mintage Rarity: R37
PR: R11
Spectral Rarity: R11
Classification: Key

Type I mintmark has a mild ridge from the top to lower serif with a radiused top serif and a slightly pointed bottom serif. Between the loops are raised areas of metal—hence the "Filled S" variety.

*Mintage minus the official Mint estimate of Type II proof cents.

1981S Proof Type II (Clear S)
Mintage: 599,000*
Mintage Rarity: R32
PR: R10
Spectral Rarity: R10
Classification: Key

Type II has a thinner middle bar than the top or bottom bars, and bulbous serifs.

*Official Mint estimate of mintage for Type II proof cents.

1982

Both "copper" and copper-plated zinc coins were manufactured in 1982.

Copper
Weight: 3.11 grams
Diameter: 19 mm
Composition: .950 copper, .050 tin and zinc

Copper-Plated Zinc
Weight: 2.50 grams
Diameter: 19 mm
Composition: Core is .992 zinc, .008 copper; plated with pure copper. Final Content is .975 zinc, .025 copper.

Timeline: Dr. Alan Goldman of the Mint (also heavily involved with the 1974 dated aluminum pattern cents) is approached by Jerry T. McDowell of the Ball Corporation of Greenville, Tennessee, with a proposal to use zinc rather than brass for the cent. After extensive testing and bean counting, the proposal is accepted by the Treasury and the contract for fabricating planchets for the new cent is awarded to none other than the Ball Corporation on July 22, 1981. The new zinc cents are scheduled to be struck on the first day of July 1981, but pre-production setbacks and a lawsuit filed by the Copper & Brass Fabricators Council delay the introduction for another year.

The main difference between the modern cents and the zinc plated steel cents of 1943 is that the steel cents were blanked from plated strips, while the modern cent is blanked from zinc strips, then the individual planchets are plated. The residual chemicals from this plating process, if not sufficiently rinsed off, can dramatically affect the coin's color and provide a catalyst for areas of corrosion under the right conditions.

Most of the general public is still unaware that the new cents are zinc thinly veiled with a layer of copper. The new zinc cents can cause serious illness, which can be life threatening if swallowed by a family pet or small child. Be sure to know what to do before this happens in your household: consult your local poison control center or your family physician.

The obverse dies are modified in September 1982—the main device (Lincoln), the lettering, and the date are made slightly smaller with shallower relief. This is done to achieve a sharper strike with lower pressure while increasing the life of the dies two-fold from approximately seven hundred thousand strikes per die pair back up to about one and a half million, which was fairly common with the old "copper" cents. It should also be noted that Philadelphia, West Point, and San Francisco all strike cents without mintmarks this year.

1982 Small Date obverse.   *Close-up of the 1982 Small Date obverse.*

1982 (Small Date)
Mintage: 10,712,525,000
Mintage Rarity: –
MSR: R6
Spectral Rarity: R6
Classification: Common

1982 (Large Date)
Mintage: Inc. above
Mintage Rarity: –
MSR: R4
Spectral Rarity: R3
Classification: Common

1982 (Small Date Zinc)
Mintage: Inc. above
Mintage Rarity: –
MSR: R5
Spectral Rarity: R5
Classification: Common

1982 Doubled Obv. Die (Small Date)
Mintage: Inc. above
Mintage Rarity: –
MSR: R7
Spectral Rarity: R6
Classification: Sub-Variety

Two varieties exist.

1982 Large Date obverse.

Close-up of the 1982 Large Date obverse.

1982 (Large Date Zinc)

Mintage: Inc. above
Mintage Rarity: –
MSR: R7
Spectral Rarity: R7
Classification: Common

1982D (Large Date)

Mintage: 10,712,525,00
Mintage Rarity: –
MSR: R5
Spectral Rarity: R5
Classification: Common

1982D (Large Date Zinc)

Mintage: Inc. above
Mintage Rarity: –
MSR: R7
Spectral Rarity: R7
Classification: Common

1982D (Small Date Zinc)

Mintage: Inc. above
Mintage Rarity: –
MSR: R6
Spectral Rarity: R6
Classification: Common

1982S Proof

Mintage: 3,857,479
Mintage Rarity: R37
PR: R9
Spectral Rarity: R9
Classification: Key

The date is of the large date variety.

1983

Mintage: 7,752,355,000
Mintage Rarity: –
MSR: R11
Spectral Rarity: R8
Classification: Common

Several minor doubled obverse dies exist, but are too common to list individually. The San Francisco Mint also produced business strike coins without a mintmark that year. Several unplated coins submitted, skewing the ratio.

1983 Doubled Obv. Die

Mintage: Inc. above
Mintage Rarity: –
MSR: R9
Spectral Rarity: R9
Classification: Sub-Variety

Four minor varieties exist. Not widely collected like the 1983 Doubled Reverse varieties.

Doubling on the 1983 Doubled Reverse Die is most visible on the words ONE CENT, AMERICA, and E PLURIBUS UNUM.

1983 Doubled Rev. Die

Mintage: Inc. above
Mintage Rarity: –
MSR: R15
Spectral Rarity: R15
Classification: Semi-Key

One of the few widely collected doubled reverse die varieties. The doubling is most visible on the words ONE CENT, AMERICA, and E PLURIBUS UNUM. This is not an axial rotation doubling, but rather an uncommon positional doubling in which the die shifted vertically. There are at least three distinct varieties.

1983D

Mintage: 6,467,199,428
Mintage Rarity: –
MSR: R7
Spectral Rarity: R7
Classification: Common

1983D Doubled Obv. Die

Mintage: Inc. above
Mintage Rarity: –
MSR: R3
Spectral Rarity: R3
Classification: Sub-Variety

1983S Proof

Mintage: 3,279,126
Mintage Rarity: R36
PR: R10
Spectral Rarity: R10
Classification: Key

1984

Mintage: 8,151,079,000
Mintage Rarity: –
MSR: R9
Spectral Rarity: R6
Classification: Common

Several specimens exist without the initials of Frank Gasparro (FG) on the reverse. These coins are only worth a slight premium, in uncirculated condition only. Several unplated coins submitted, skewing the ratio.

1984 Doubled Obv. Die

Mintage: Inc. above
Mintage Rarity: –
MSR: R16
Spectral Rarity: R16
Classification: Semi-Key

The 1984 Doubled Die has a partial earlobe showing directly below Lincoln's ear and slightly to the left. The partial earlobe is the visible remains of a previous strike on the working die from the master die. The subsequent strike obliterated most of the design imparted by the initial strike. Five varieties exist.

Notice the partial earlobe directly below and slightly to the left of Lincoln's ear on the 1984 Doubled Obverse Die.

1984D

Mintage: 5,569,238,906
Mintage Rarity: –
MSR: R8
Spectral Rarity: R7
Classification: Common

1984D Doubled Obv. Die

Mintage: Inc. above
Mintage Rarity: –
MSR: R4
Spectral Rarity: R4-
Classification: Sub-Variety

1984S Proof

Mintage: 3,065,110
Mintage Rarity: R36
PR: R10
Spectral Rarity: R10
Classification: Key

(L) **Timeline:** Coinage operations are temporarily suspended at the West Point facility because the Gramm-Rudman Act legislates cutbacks and cost saving measures.

1985
Mintage: 5,648,489,887*
Mintage Rarity: –
MSR: R7
Spectral Rarity: R6
Classification: Common

   *696,585,000 were actually minted at West Point.

1985D
Mintage: 5,287,399,926
Mintage Rarity: –
MSR: R9
Spectral Rarity: R8
Classification: Common

1985D/D
Mintage: Inc. above
Mintage Rarity: –
MSR: –
Spectral Rarity: –
Classification: RPM Sub-Variety

1985S Proof
Mintage: 3,362,821
Mintage Rarity: R36
PR: R9
Spectral Rarity: R9
Classification: Key

   Beginning in 1985 for proof coinage and 1990 for business strikes, the mintmark was added directly to the hub rather than the individual working dies. Every working die made with that hub will produce cents with the mintmark in the exact same position.

1986
Mintage: 4,491,395,493
Mintage Rarity: –
MSR: R6
Spectral Rarity: R5
Classification: Common

1986 Doubled Obv. Die
Mintage: Inc. above
Mintage Rarity: –
MSR: R3
Spectral Rarity: R3
Classification: Sub-Variety

1986D

Mintage: 4,442,866,698
Mintage Rarity: –
MSR: R8
Spectral Rarity: R7
Classification: Common

1986S Proof

Mintage: 3,010,497
Mintage Rarity: R36
PR: R9
Spectral Rarity: R9
Classification: Key

1987

Mintage: 4,682,466,931
Mintage Rarity: –
MSR: R7
Spectral Rarity: R7
Classification: Common

1987 Doubled Obv. Die

Mintage: Inc. above
Mintage Rarity: –
MSR: R5
Spectral Rarity: R5
Classification: Sub-Variety

Two varieties exist.

1987D

Mintage: 4,879,389,514
Mintage Rarity: –
MSR: R7
Spectral Rarity: R6
Classification: Common

1987S Proof

Mintage: 3,792,233
Mintage Rarity: R37
PR: R10
Spectral Rarity: R10
Classification: Key

1988

Mintage: 6,092,810,000
Mintage Rarity: –
MSR: R6
Spectral Rarity: R4
Classification: Common

1988 Doubled Obv. Die
Mintage: Inc. above
Mintage Rarity: –
MSR: R6
Spectral Rarity: R6
Classification: Sub-Variety

Two varieties exist.

1988D
Mintage: 5,253,740,443
Mintage Rarity: –
MSR: R6
Spectral Rarity: R6
Classification: Common

1988D Doubled Obv. Die
Mintage: Inc. above
Mintage Rarity: –
MSR: R4
Spectral Rarity: R4
Classification: Sub-Variety

1988D/D
Mintage: Inc. above
Mintage Rarity: –
MSR: R3
Spectral Rarity: R3
Classification: RPM Sub-Variety

1988S Proof
Mintage: 3,262,948
Mintage Rarity: R36
PR: R10
Spectral Rarity: R10
Classification: Key

1989
Mintage: 7,261,535,000
Mintage Rarity: –
MSR: R8
Spectral Rarity: R7
Classification: Common

1989D
Mintage: 5,345,467,111
Mintage Rarity: –
MSR: R6
Spectral Rarity: R6
Classification: Common

1989S Proof
Mintage: 3,215,728
Mintage Rarity: R36
PR: R10
Spectral Rarity: R10
Classification: Key

🕐 **Timeline:** The U.S. Mint decides to "punch" the mintmark directly into the cent hubs rather than the thousands of working dies manufactured for the branch mints each year.

1990
Mintage: 6,851,765,000
Mintage Rarity: –
MSR: R8
Spectral Rarity: R7
Classification: Common

1990D
Mintage: 4,922,894,533
Mintage Rarity: –
MSR: R9
Spectral Rarity: R9
Classification: Common

1990S Proof
Mintage: 3,299,559
Mintage Rarity: R36
PR: R9
Spectral Rarity: R9
Classification: Key

1990S "No S" Proof
Mintage: 3,555*
Mintage Rarity: R19
PR: R3
Spectral Rarity: R3
Classification: Key

A very rare and unique type of minting variety. When the hubs were being prepared, a mint employee forgot to "punch" the mintmark into the hubs, which became standard operating procedure in 1985. The proof cents have at least fourteen people working with or examining the dies and the coins, including the person making the hubs and the working dies, the press operators, the inspectors, and the packaging line personnel,

This "No S" variety was actually discovered by a coin collector.

who actually assemble the proof sets. This variety was discovered not by a mint employee, but by a collector. When news reached the Mint about the "No S" proof cent, the Mint inspected all of the proof sets awaiting shipment.

*An additional 145 no-mintmark cents were discovered and destroyed by the Mint.

1991
Mintage: 5,165,940,000
Mintage Rarity: –
MSR: R8
Spectral Rarity: R7
Classification: Common

1991D
Mintage: 4,158,442,076
Mintage Rarity: –
MSR: R9
Spectral Rarity: R9
Classification: Common

1991S Proof
Mintage: 2,867,787
Mintage Rarity: R36
PR: R8
Spectral Rarity: R8
Classification: Key

1992
Mintage: 4,648,905,000
Mintage Rarity: –
MSR: R7
Spectral Rarity: R7
Classification: Common

1992D
Mintage: 4,468,673,300
Mintage Rarity: –
MSR: R8
Spectral Rarity: R8
Classification: Common

1992S Proof
Mintage: 4,176,544
Mintage Rarity: R37
PR: R10
Spectral Rarity: R10
Classification: Key

1993
Mintage: 5,684,705,000
Mintage Rarity: –
MSR: R8
Spectral Rarity: R7
Classification: Common

1993D
Mintage: 6,426,650,571
Mintage Rarity: –
MSR: R7
Spectral Rarity: R7
Classification: Common

1993S Proof
Mintage: 2,569,882
Mintage Rarity: R36
PR: R9
Spectral Rarity: R9
Classification: Key

1994
Mintage: –
Mintage Rarity: –
MSR: R9
Spectral Rarity: R9
Classification: Common

1994D
Mintage: –
Mintage Rarity: –
MSR: R7
Spectral Rarity: R6
Classification: Common

1994S Proof
Mintage: –
Mintage Rarity: –
PR: R10
Spectral Rarity: R10
Classification: Key

1995
Mintage: –
Mintage Rarity: –
MSR: R7
Spectral Rarity: R7
Classification: Common

1995 Doubled Obv. Die
Mintage: Inc. above
Mintage Rarity: –
MSR: R19
Spectral Rarity: R19
Classification: Sub-variety

This latest doubled die features strong doubling on LIBERTY and on the words IN GOD. The doubling is more evident on the left side of the coin than the right. The doubling shows that a slight CCW axial rotation occurred during the hubbing process. It is too early yet to tell if this variety has the staying power of similar doubled dies like the 1969S or the 1984, but the numbers so far indicate that it is far more common than any other doubled die in the series.

1995D
Mintage: –
Mintage Rarity: –
MSR: R6
Spectral Rarity: R6
Classification: Common

1995S Proof
Mintage: –
Mintage Rarity: –
PR: R7
Spectral Rarity: R7
Classification: Key

Notice the strong doubling on LIBERTY and on the words IN GOD. Doubling is more evident on the left side of the 1995 Doubled Obverse Die coin.

A close-up of the doubling.

GLOSSARY

ALLOY: A mixture of two or more metals, typically with the most abundant metal first; e.g., cupronickel alloy.

ALTERED DATE: A date on a coin that has been altered to make the coin appear to be one of greater numismatic value; e.g., 1944 Lincoln Cent changed to a 19 14 Lincoln Cent.

AMERICAN NUMISMATIC ASSOCIATION: A national organization chartered by Congress for the purpose of educating the public in matters of coins, paper monies, and exonumia.

ANNEAL: A process used to soften metal by heating before the striking process.

BAG MARKS: Marks on uncirculated coins caused by contact with other coins in the same bag, hopper, or bin. Also referred to as CONTACT MARKS.

BASE METAL: Nonprecious metal such as zinc, steel, copper, and so on.

BLANK: A round metal disk that will be made into a coin. Also referred to as a PLANCHET.

BLANKING: The process of stamping or punching out BLANKS or PLANCHETS from metal strips.

BOURSE: A specific area where coins are bought and sold at coin shows or conventions.

BRASS: An alloy of copper and zinc.

BROKEN-OUT: A slang term used to describe a coin that was removed from a third-party grading service holder or SLAB.

BRONZE: An alloy of copper and tin.

BURNISH: The process of polishing PLANCHETS for PROOF coins using metal beads.

BUSINESS STRIKE: A coin made for general circulation, as opposed to PROOF coins.

CABINET FRICTION: Tiny scratches typically in the same direction on the highest portions of a coin caused by the sliding of the coin against parts of the album or cabinet tray in which it is housed.

CAVITATION: A sinking or bowl-shaped effect resulting from multiple die strikes.

CHERRY PICK: Acquiring only the best coins from circulation or from dealers.

CLASSIFICATION: The generally agreed upon term used most often to describe a coin's condition or rarity, e.g., SEMI-KEY, KEY, SUB-VARIETY, and so on.

COIN: A small metal disk used in exchange for goods or services.

COLLAR: Also known as the third die; a heavy metal ring that holds the PLANCHET in place and forces the metal of the PLANCHET to cold flow into the devices of the obverse and reverse dies as it is being struck.

CONDITION: Also known as GRADE.

CONTACT MARKS: Marks on uncirculated coins caused by contact with other coins in the same bag, hopper, or bin. Also referred to as BAG MARKS.

COUNTERFEIT: An imitation coin manufactured to deceive collectors or to be used for monetary trade.

DENOMINATION: The face value of a coin.

DEVICE: The main design or motif on a coin; e.g., the bust of Lincoln.

DIE: A hardened piece of steel, typically with an incuse design, used to strike the PLANCHETS to form coins.

DIE BREAK: An area of raised metal on the surface of a coin caused by a broken, yet retained die.

DIE CRACK: A fine line of raised metal on the surface of a coin caused by a crack in the die.

DIPPING: Immersing a coin in a weak solution of acid and water to remove tarnish or dirt from the coin's surface.

DOUBLE DIE: Any coin that has the appearance of a DOUBLED DIE due to machine doubling, abrasion doubling, and so on.

DOUBLED DIE: Any coin that is struck from a die that was rotated during the hubbing process.

EDGE: The curved surface (thickness) perpendicular to the OBVERSE and REVERSE of a coin. Often confused with the RIM of a coin.

ELECTROTYPE: A COUNTERFEIT process used to make coins using electroplating.

ERRORS: Also known as minting varieties. Most are the result of using DIES past their intended duty life.

EXONUMIA: The hobby of collecting coin-like objects such as medals, tokens, and badges.

FACE: Usually refers to the OBVERSE of a coin, but can also refer to the REVERSE.

FACE VALUE: The amount or DENOMINATION of a coin for monetary trade.

FIELD: The "flat" areas of the obverse and reverse of a coin, less the DEVICES and INSCRIPTIONS.

FLIP: A two-inch by two-inch coin holder that is made of a soft pliable plastic.

FLOW LINES: Microscopic lines on a coin's surface produced as the metal of the PLANCHET is cold flowed during the striking process. Also referred to as MINT LUSTER.

FROST: A grainy effect on the DEVICES and INSCRIPTIONS caused by new or specially prepared DIES; also referred to as cameo effect.

GRADE: A measure of wear or surface detractions on a coin; also known as CONDITION.

HAIRLINES: Tiny random scratches on the surface of a coin.

HOARD: A large haphazard collection of coins, typically all of the same denomination.

HUB: The "die" used to make WORKING DIES that actually strike the PLANCHETS into coins. The hub has the same relief as the coins.

IMPAIRED: A proof coin that was released into circulation and shows evidence of wear.

IMPRESSION: A reverse image of a finished coin as seen on a WORKING DIE.

INCUSE: The part of a DIE or COIN that is below the surface; opposite of relief.

INSCRIPTION: The lettering on a coin; also referred to as a LEGEND.

KEY: A relatively rare coin in any grade usually with a low mintage, e.g., 1909S VDB

LEGEND: The lettering on a coin's OBVERSE or REVERSE.

LOUPE: A magnifying glass that folds in on itself, protecting the lens from damage.

LUSTER: The reflectivity of a coin's surface caused by the light reflecting off the minute FLOW LINES on the coin's surface; also referred to as MINT LUSTER.

MASTER DIE: The die used to make HUBS.

MATTE PROOF: A coin that is struck in the conventional manner as regular PROOF coins, but is processed after being struck. Minted from 1909 to 1916.

MINTAGE: The total quantity of coins produced for a given mint and year.

MINTAGE RARITY: A number representing a range of mintages.

MINT LUSTER: The reflectivity of a coin's surface caused by the light reflecting off the minute FLOW LINES on the coin's surface.

MINTMARK: A letter on the cents designating where the coin was minted. (D for Denver, S for San Francisco, and no mintmark for Philadelphia.)

MINT SET: A mint packaged set of each denomination of uncirculated coins struck for circulation that year.

MINT STATE (MS): A coin that has not been used by the general public since it left the mint and thus shows no sign of wear.

MINT STATE RARITY (MSR): A number designating the quantity of uncirculated coins submitted to third-party grading services for a given mint and year.

MOTTO: The words "IN GOD WE TRUST" and "E PLURIBUS UNUM."

MYLAR: A chemically inert plastic used in the production of "flips."

NUMISMATICS: The study of coins and related topics.

OBVERSE (OBV.): The "front" side of a coin, usually referred to as "heads." Typically, the obverse contains the date that the coin was minted.

OVERDATE: Numerals in the date that are superimposed over numerals that are not the same, e.g., 1942/41.

OVERMINTMARK (OMM): A mintmark that is placed on top of a mintmark from a different mint, e.g., D/S.

PATINA: The natural coloration of a coin caused by oxidation over a period of time; also referred to as TONING.

PATTERN: A sample coin that is being proposed for production.

PENNY: An English coin. Not to be confused with the American cent.

PITTING: A concentrated chemical reaction creating small unsightly holes in the surface of a copper coin.

PLANCHET: A round metal disk that will be made into a coin; also referred to as a BLANK.

POPULATION REPORT: A census put out by several third-party grading services, indicating the quantity, grade, and variety of coins that were submitted to date.

PROOF: A coin made from specially prepared PLANCHETS that are struck at least twice from special dies, creating sharp images and mirrored FIELDS. These coins are typically sold through the Mint to collectors.

PROOF-LIKE: Coins that are struck with Very Early Die State dies. These general circulation coins are the first coins produced by new dies and may show cameo effects on the devices, and have mirrored fields.

PROOF SET: A mint packaged set of each denomination of PROOF coins struck that year. Typically sold through the Mint to collectors.

RAW: A coin that has not been submitted and ENCAPSULATED in an airtight plastic holder by a third-party grading or authentication service.

RELIEF: The raised portion of the design or DEVICE on a coin that extends above the FIELDS.

REVERSE (REV.): The side of the coin opposite the OBVERSE, commonly referred to as the "tails" side of the coin.

RIDDLER: A vibrating screen used to separate good and defective PLANCHETS.

RIM: The raised border around the periphery of the OBVERSE and REVERSE of a coin.

SEMI-KEY: A relatively rare coin in any grade, usually with a moderately low mintage. Not as rare as a KEY; e.g., 1931S.

SERIES: A set of coins with all possible mintmark and date combinations, such as the Lincoln Memorial Cents from 1959 to date.

SLAB: A slang term referring to an ENCAPSULATED coin.

SLEEPER: An undervalued coin with a potential to dramatically increase in value; e.g., all Lincoln matte proofs.

SLIDER: A coin that was graded one grade higher than it should have been. A very subjective term.

SPECIAL MINT SET (SMS): A mint packaged set of uncirculated coins sold to collectors 1965-1967. Although minted in San Francisco, these coins do not contain a mintmark, and were issued in lieu of proof sets.

SPECIFIC GRAVITY: The weight of a material (coin) compared to an equally displaced volume of water.

SPECTRAL RARITY: A number designating the quantity of uncirculated coins with full MINT LUSTER submitted to third-party grading services for a given mint and year.

SPOTTING: Typically small isolated areas of oxidation on the surface of a copper coin, commonly caused by a reaction with sulfur and/or human oil from the fingertips.

SUB-VARIETY: A coin that, by consensus, is not needed to form a "complete set"; e.g., 1955 Poor Man's Double Die.

TONING: The natural coloration of a coin caused by oxidation over a period of time; also referred to as PATINA.

UNCIRCULATED (Unc.): A coin that has not been used by the general public since it left the mint and thus shows no sign of wear.

VERDIGRIS: An oily green film or crust that forms on the surface of a coin (usually near the rim) as a result of a chemical reaction between the copper and an acid.

VICTOR DAVID BRENNER: The designer of the OBVERSE and REVERSE of the Lincoln Cent (1871-1924).

WHIZZING: A process whereby toning and/or oxidation is removed, usually done by novices with a pencil eraser to achieve polished surfaces.

WORKING DIE: The DIE used to strike PLANCHETS into COINS.

WORKING HUB: A tool that has the same relief as the finished coin and is used to make WORKING DIES.

NUMISMATIC RELATED CLUBS AND ORGANIZATIONS

American Numismatic Association
818 N. Cascade Avenue
Colorado Springs, CO 80903-3279
719-632-2646

American Numismatic Society
Broadway at 155th Street
New York, NY 10032
212-234-3130

Director of the Mint
633 3rd St. NW
Washington, DC 20220
202-376-0560

San Francisco Mint
Duboce Ave. & Market St.
San Francisco, CA 94103
415-556-6707

U.S. Mint, Customer Service Center
10001 Aerospace Dr.
Lanham, MD 20706

U.S. Mint (Denver)
Colfax and Delaware Sts.
Denver, CO 80204
303-844-4289

U.S. Mint (Philadelphia)
5th St. at Independence Mall
Philadelphia, PA 19106
215-597-2063

U.S. Mint (West Point)
West Point, NY 10996
914-887-9659

ANA MEMBERSHIP APPLICATION

Application for membership in the
American Numismatic Association

Choose One:
- __ Regular   __ Senior   __ Junior
- __ Associate   __ Club   __ Life

See reverse for membership rate schedule

Present or former ANA# (if any)_____

__ Mr.   __ Mrs.   __ Ms.   __ Club

_____
Name (please print)

_____
Street

_____
City   State   Zip

_____
Birthdate (required for Junior and Senior Membership)

ANA Bylaws require the publication of each applicant's name and state.

____ Check here if you DO NOT want your name and address forwarded to the ANA Representative in your area.

____ Check here if you would like your name provided to numismatic-related companies.

I agree to abide by the American Numismatic Association's bylaws and Code of Ethics which require the publication of each applicant's name and state.

_____
Signature of Applicant

_____
Signature of Parent/Guardian (required for Junior Applicant)

Amount Paid_____

Method of Payment:

__ Cash   __ Check   __ Money Order

__ Master Card   __ VISA   __ American Express

_____   _____
Credit Card Account No.(all digits)   Expiration Date

_____
Signature of Card Holder (required)

Return application with payment to:
American Numismatic Association
818 North Cascade Avenue
Colorado Springs, CO 80903-3279
PHONE : 719/632-2646
FAX : 719/634-4085
INTERNET: anamem@athena.csdco.com

Foreign applications must be accompanied by U.S. funds drawn on a U.S. Bank

The back side of the application, showing membership dues, is illustrated on the next page.

143

MEMBERSHIP DUES SCHEDULE

Regular Member (Adult)	$ 35.00*
Regular 3-Year	$ 79.00
Regular 5-Year	$ 130.00
Senior Member (65 years and over)	$ 31.00*
Senior 3-Year	$ 69.00
Senior 5-Year	$ 110.00
Junior Member (under 18 years of age)	$ 11.00
Junior 3-Year**	$ 30.00
Junior 5-Year**	$ 45.00
Associate Member (Spouse, Son or Daughter of Regular, Senior or Life Member)	$ 4.00
Associate 3-Year	$ 10.00
Associate 5-Year	$ 16.00
Club Membership (Group of collectors that join as a Coin Club)	$ 39.00*
Club 3-Year	$ 99.00
Club 5-Year	$ 165.00
Foreign Regular Member (Adult)	$ 42.00*
Foreign Regular 3-Year	$ 108.00
Foreign Regular 5-Year	$ 180.00
Foreign Senior Member (65 years and over)	$ 38.00*
Foreign Senior 3-Year	$ 96.00
Foreign Senior 5-Year	$ 160.00
Foreign Junior Member (under 18 years)	$ 11.00
Foreign Junior 3-Year **	$ 33.00
Foreign Junior 5-Year **	$ 55.00
Foreign Associate Member	$ 4.00
Foreign Associate 3-Year	$ 12.00
Foreign Associate 5-Year	$ 20.00

* Subsequent years will be $6 less

** Must be under 18 years of age during entire 3- or 5-year period

Foreign applications must be accompanied by U.S. Funds drawn on a U.S. bank.

LIFE MEMBERSHIP PROGRAM

Life Membership	$ 750.00
Senior Life Membership (65 years and older)	$ 500.00
Golden Life Membership (50 year member)	$ 250.00
Special rates available for Associate Life members (Spouses of Current Life members)	
Club Life Membership	$1250.00

An installment plan is available for Life Membership applicants.